Collins

AQA GCSE 9-1
Psychology
Workbook

Sally White

Preparing for the GCSE Exam

Revision That Really Works

Experts have found that there are two techniques that help you to retain and recall information and consistently produce better results in exams compared to other revision techniques.

It really isn't rocket science either – you simply need to:

- **test yourself** on each topic as many times as possible
- **leave a gap** between the test sessions.

Three Essential Revision Tips

1. **Use Your Time Wisely**

   - Allow yourself plenty of time.
   - Try to start revising six months before your exams – it's more effective and less stressful.
   - Don't waste time re-reading the same information over and over again – it's not effective!

2. **Make a Plan**

   - Identify all the topics you need to revise.
   - Plan at least five sessions for each topic.
   - One hour should be ample time to test yourself on the key ideas for a topic.
   - Spread out the practice sessions for each topic – the optimum time to leave between each session is about one month but, if this isn't possible, just make the gaps as big as realistically possible.

3. **Test Yourself**

   - Methods for testing yourself include: quizzes, practice questions, flashcards, past papers, explaining a topic to someone else, etc.
   - Don't worry if you get an answer wrong – provided you check what the correct answer is, you are more likely to get the same or similar questions right in future!

Visit **collins.co.uk/collinsGCSErevision** for more information about the benefits of these techniques, and for further guidance on how to plan ahead and make them work for you.

Command Words Used in Exam Questions

This table shows the meanings of some of the most commonly used command words in GCSE exam questions.

Command word	Meaning
Calculate...	A calculation needs to be carried out
Compare...	Give a balanced answer of similarities and differences
Describe...	Give an account of
Evaluate...	A description is needed but with the emphasis on a conclusion
Explain...	Give detailed reasons for your answer
Identify...	Be able to recognise the answer, often from the information given
Name...	Be able to give a recognised technical term
Outline...	Give an overview of the main characteristics

Contents

Cognition and Behaviour

Social Context and Behaviour

Exam Papers

Memory

Where space is not provided, write your answers on a separate piece of paper.

1 | Alina and George are revising for their GCSE Psychology exam. Alina finds revising much easier once she has mastered all the concepts in the topics and understands what they mean. George draws diagrams of information such as mind maps.

Which types of encoding are Alina and George using?

Alina _____ [1]

George _____ [1]

2 Define the following terms:

Encoding [2]

_____

_____

Storage [2]

_____

_____

Retrieval [2]

_____

_____

3 Which of the following statements about encoding are correct?
Shade **two** boxes. [2]

   A An example of visual encoding is if you are asked to mentally picture your house. ◯

   B An example of semantic encoding is knowing the capital city of France. ◯

   C An example of visual encoding is repeating a poem you have read. ◯

   D An example of acoustic coding is storing information by meaning. ◯

4 Outline **two** features of storage. [2]

_____

_____

Memory

5 Explain how different types of retrieval can be used, referring to the example below. **[6]**

> Bobby cannot remember all the names of the football teams in his league unless his friend gives him the first letter of the name. Anil, who plays in the same team, says he can easily pick out all of the teams in their league if he is shown a full list of all team names in all leagues. Nick suggests he needs no help whatsoever.

6 Using research evidence, evaluate semantic, procedural and episodic memories. **[5]**

7 Describe the multi-store model of memory. **[6]**

8 Explain **one** strength of the multi-store model of memory. **[2]**

....

....

9 According to the multi-store model, what is the duration of the short-term memory? **[1]**

....

10
> Dayna and Archie had both been taught the names of famous psychologists in chronological order of when they were influential. They were told by their teacher they would be tested the next day and they had to recall them in the correct order. They both revised that evening. Dayna had her psychology lesson first in the morning so she sat the test first. Archie did not sit his test until after break, after his Spanish lesson.

a) According to interference theory, who is more likely to have forgotten some of the names – Dayna or Archie?

.... **[1]**

b) When analysing the class results, the teacher noticed there was a pattern of which names were easily recalled and which ones were forgotten. It was noted that the students were more likely to correctly recall the first few names and the last few names but the names in the middle were likely to be forgotten or mixed up.

What is the term used to describe this pattern of results?

.... **[1]**

11 Outline **one** difference between short-term and long-term memory. **[2]**

....

....

12 Murdock investigated the effects of serial position on recall.

How does this study support the multi-store model of memory? **[4]**

Memory

13 Which of the following statements about Murdock's study are incorrect?
Shade **two** boxes. **[2]**

A Murdock randomly selected words from the 4000 most common words in English. ◯

B The independent variable (IV) was the position of a word in the list. ◯

C The dependent variable (DV) was the words recalled in serial position. ◯

D The study used an independent measures design. ◯

E The study was a field experiment. ◯

14 What is meant by 'effort after meaning'? **[2]**

....

....

15 Using an example, describe the reconstructive theory of memory. **[3]**

16 Describe the findings of Bartlett's 'War of the Ghosts' study. **[3]**

17

Emilia was telling her friend Ellie that she was asked to participate in a psychology experiment on memory. She told Ellie that the researchers were really strict with their instructions and all of the participants were asked to do exactly the same thing. However, whilst she was participating, she kept trying to work out what they were really testing.

a) What type of experiment did Emilia participate in? **[1]**

....

b) What is **one** weakness of the method that Emilia is referring to? **[2]**

....

....

18 What is meant by false memories? Give an example. **[3]**

19 You have been asked to investigate accuracy of memory with reference to context of recall. Describe how you would design an experiment to do this. **[6]**

You need to include:

- The procedure – what participants could do to test the accuracy of memory and context of recall

- A suitable hypothesis for your experiment

- The results that you expect to find.

Perception

Where space is not provided, write your answers on a separate piece of paper.

1 Outline the difference between sensation and perception. [4]

2 What are monocular depth cues? [2]

....

....

3 Which **two** of the following are monocular depth cues? Shade **two** boxes. [2]

A Convergence ◯   B Linear perspective ◯

C Retinal disparity ◯   D Height in plane ◯

E Motion parallax ◯

4 What are binocular depth cues? [2]

....

....

5 Sketch the Ponzo illusion. [1]

6 Outline how psychologists would explain the Ponzo illusion. [3]

Perception

7 A researcher showed male and female participants the Kanizsa triangle (**Figure 1**). They were asked to write down their perception of what they saw – a white triangle on top of another triangle, incomplete circles or an incomplete triangle. The researcher split the results into male and female responses.

Figure 1.

The results are shown in **Table 1**.

	White triangle	Incomplete circles	Incomplete triangle	Total
Males	100	70	30	200
Females	140	60	20	220
Total	240	130	50	420

a) Draw a suitable graph to represent the data in **Table 1**.
   Provide a suitable title and fully label your graph.   [4]

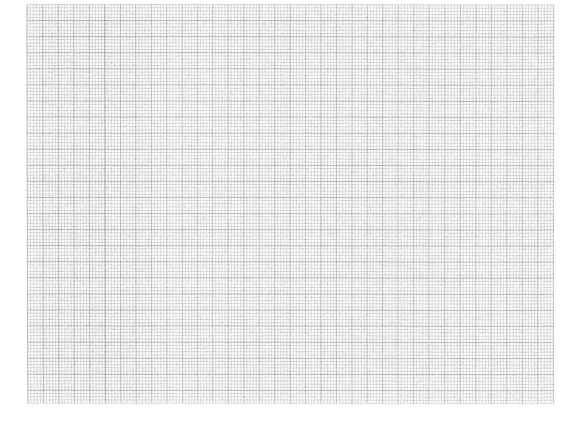

b) Calculate the ratio of males to females. Show your workings. **[2]**

c) 50% of the men in the study perceived **Figure 1** to be a white triangle. Calculate the percentage of women (to three significant figures) who also perceived the illusion to be a white triangle. Show your workings. **[2]**

d) Which of the following is the correct fraction of both males and females who saw **Figure 1** as a white triangle?
Shade **one** box only. **[1]**

A $\frac{1}{7}$ ○   B $\frac{3}{4}$ ○

C $\frac{1}{2}$ ○   D $\frac{4}{7}$ ○

E $\frac{2}{7}$ ○

8 What is meant by perceptual set? **[2]**

9 How is perceptual set affected by culture? **[2]**

10 Researchers advertised for a group of vegetarians to participate in a word search study. There were two conditions. Condition one included a word search of twenty food neutral words, such as crisps and pear. Condition two contained twenty words of food associated with meat, such as stew. Participants took part in both conditions on different days. Participants were timed on the time it took them to complete the task.

Using the theory of perceptual set and emotion, explain what results the researcher would expect to find. **[3]**

11 Why can findings of studies looking at the effects of emotions on perception be unreliable? **[2]**

12 Evaluate Gilchrist and Nesberg's study on how motivation affects perception. **[4]**

13 Describe the findings of the Bruner and Minturn study of perceptual set.   **[6]**

14 Participants volunteered to take part in research where they were asked to look at pictures flashed on a screen. Some pictures, such as a piece of fruit, were neutral and some were more anxiety-inducing, such as a scene from a disaster. As soon as they saw the picture they had to say what it depicted out loud. Their anxiety was measured using a galvanic skin response machine which would record their anxiety through the amount of electrical activity caused by sweat. It was found that it took longer for participants to say what the anxiety-inducing pictures showed than the neutral pictures and they produced a higher skin conductance (more anxiety) with the anxiety-inducing pictures.

What is the name of the perceptual set?

Explain the findings of the above study.   **[4]**

15 Explain why the data in this study is primary data.   **[2]**

Development

Where space is not provided, write your answers on a separate piece of paper.

1 Which of the following is the part of the brain where all of our thinking and processing takes place? Shade **one** box only. **[1]**

   A Brain stem ◯

   B Cerebellum ◯

   C Cortex ◯

   D Thalamus ◯

2 What is meant by automatic functions? Give **one** example. **[3]**

3 Emilia is four and is learning to hop. Which part of the brain is involved in this activity? Shade **one** box only. **[1]**

   A Brain stem ◯

   B Cerebellum ◯

   C Cortex ◯

   D Thalamus ◯

4 Smoking is just one factor that may affect a growing brain. This is an example of nurture. What is meant by nurture? **[2]**

5 Give **one** other factor that could be considered nurture. **[1]**

6 A midwife is interested in brain development in the womb. She delivered information programmes warning women about the dangers of smoking, particularly if they were going to have children. She then conducted a study to find out if her information programme had had an effect. She asked women attending the clinic, who had attended her information programme, if they would take part in her study.

At the end of the study she found the following results in **Table 1**:

Table 1. Percentage of mothers who smoked before pregnancy and stopped during pregnancy.

Smoked before pregnancy	Stopped smoking during pregnancy
87	69

Calculate the percentage decrease of mothers who stopped smoking, to two significant figures. Show your workings. **[3]**

7 With reference to the above study, which sampling method did the midwife use? **[2]**

_____

_____

8 What is meant by nature? **[2]**

_____

_____

9 **a)** Label the areas of the brain A, B, C and D. **[4]**

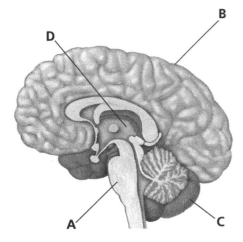

b) Write A, B, C and D in the boxes to match each area to its function.

Autonomic functions such as breathing and heartbeat	
Precise physical movement/coordinates actions	
Cognition/thinking/perception/memory processes	
Some sensory processing/relaying signals to the cerebral cortex	

[4]

10 Describe Piaget's concepts of assimilation and accommodation. **[4]**

11 Keshav was complaining that his teacher was unhelpful in class when he was struggling to understand the work. Another student, Seb, liked the teacher and felt Keshav had been messing around during the lesson and that was why he struggled. When Seb wanted the teacher's help but didn't get it, he changed his mind about the teacher.

Is Seb showing an example of assimilation or accommodation? Explain your answer. **[4]**

12 Daisy's aunt pours a drink for Daisy into a tall, narrow beaker. Daisy's sister, Maya, also wants a drink but her drink (the same amount as Daisy's) is poured into a short, wide beaker. Maya laughs and says she has more drink than Daisy. Daisy just smiles.

Development

a) Using your knowledge of conservation, which sister is the youngest?   **[1]**

b) Using your knowledge of conservation, how old is the eldest sister likely to be?   **[1]**

c) Which stage is the youngest sister likely to be at?   **[1]**

13 Which **one** of the following suggests that development happens in stages? Shade **one** box only.   **[1]**

A   Willingham   ◯

B   Dweck   ◯

C   Piaget   ◯

14 Evaluate McGarrigle and Donaldson's naughty teddy study.   **[5]**

15 What is meant by egocentrism?   **[2]**

16 Briefly describe how Piaget studied egocentrism in young children.   **[3]**

17 Hughes investigated the development of conservation in the policeman doll study. Describe this study.

Evaluate the research method used in the Hughes study.   **[9]**

18 Complete the table below by writing the stage or age of cognitive development according to Piaget.   **[4]**

Stage	Age
Sensorimotor	
	2-7 years
	7-11 years
Formal operational	

19 Briefly outline the sensorimotor stage and the pre-operational stage of cognitive development.   **[4]**

20 Outline the role of Piaget's theory in education.   **[4]**

21 Outline **two** weaknesses of Piaget's theory.   **[4]**

Development

22 According to Dweck, what is a fixed mindset?   [2]

_____

_____

23 According to Dweck, what is a growth mindset?   [2]

_____

_____

24
Darragh believes he isn't very good at school and he doesn't worry when he is absent. Adam doesn't like being away from school as he knows he will have to catch up on missed work if he wants to do well.

Name the mindset that each student has.   [2]

_____

_____

25 Discuss how praise and self-efficacy could be used to have an impact on both Darragh and Adam at school.   [6]

26 A school asked their sixth form students which learning style they preferred.
Sketch a suitable diagram to represent the data in **Table 2**.   [4]

Table 2.

A	B	C
Preferred listening and talking	Preferred diagrams, mind maps, images	No preference
45%	35%	20%

Research

Where space is not provided, write your answers on a separate piece of paper.

1 How can a random sample be selected? [2]

2 What is **one** advantage of a random sample? [2]

3 a) A researcher wanted to choose participants for a study using systematic sampling from an alphabetical register of adults aged over eighteen and working in a college. A colleague suggested stratified sampling would be better. Explain why stratified sampling should be more representative of the target population. [4]

b) The researcher gathered their stratified sample of participants but was now concerned about how they could allocate participants to an independent groups design study. Explain how they could do this. [2]

c) A different colleague then identified problems with using an independent groups design. Outline **one** problem the researcher might encounter and suggest **one** way this problem could be addressed. [4]

d) The researcher had allocated their participants into two experimental conditions. The study was looking at the effects of alcohol on driving performance. One condition had a 300ml bottle of beer and the other did not. Identify **one** ethical issue with this study and explain how this issue could be overcome. [4]

e) Identify the independent variable in this study. [2]

f) How could the dependent variable be operationalised? [2]

4 In both conditions the researcher used a driving hazard video test but was concerned about extraneous variables. What are potential extraneous variables in this study? [3]

5 Write a suitable hypothesis for the effects of alcohol on driving performance. [3]

6 The results of the study were presented in **Table 1**.

Table 1.

	Alcohol	No Alcohol
Median	5	6.5
Range	6	3

[3]

a) What does the range tell us about the difference in the driving performance between the two conditions? [2]

_____

_____

b) Outline **one** problem in using the range to present results. [2]

_____

_____

7 A researcher gathered students for a study on memory. The students were gathered in the common room at break and asked if they would take part in the study. Those that agreed were asked to meet in the psychology lab at 1pm to participate. On arrival they were asked to sign a consent form.

a) What does a consent form include? [2]

_____

_____

b) Name the sampling technique that the researcher used. [1]

_____

8 After signing the consent form, participants were asked to look at a set of photographs of people's faces. After twenty minutes they were shown a second set of photographs, including the faces they had already seen and some new ones. The participants were asked to identify if they had seen the faces previously. They had a 90% accuracy in recognition.

a) Which research method has been used in this study? [1]

_____

b) Outline **one** strength and **one** weakness of using this method. [4]

9 In a different study, a staged incident occurred, whereby participants witnessed a 'robbery' amongst an audience at a school play. A person entered the stage and 'stole' a valuable ring being used in a scene. The audience were individually interviewed about the description of the 'thief'. In this study, 25% accuracy was recorded regarding important features of the perpetrator.

a) Which research method has been used in this study? [1]

b) Outline **one** strength and **one** weakness of using this method. [4]

c) Explain the main differences between the two studies. [4]

10 Which **one** of the following is an example of a qualitative research method? Shade **one** box only. [1]

A Laboratory experiment ◯

B Correlational study ◯

C Case study ◯

D Field experiment ◯

11 What is the purpose of random assignment in an experimental study? Shade **one** box only. [1]

A To ensure the sample is representative of the population ◯

B To increase the generalisability of results ◯

C To control for the effects of extraneous variables ◯

D To determine causation ◯

12 A researcher is studying a relationship between two co-variables. What is this research method called? Shade **one** box only. [1]

A Correlation ◯

B Laboratory experiment ◯

C Case study ◯

D Field experiment ◯

13 Outline **one** difference between primary and secondary data. [2]

Research

14 Some students completed a psychology test.

Their scores out of 100 were: 75, 82, 90, 88, 95, 64, 59, 67, 52, 41, 75, 53, 72

  a) Work out the median score. Show your workings.   [2]

  b) Work out the range of the scores. Show your workings.   [2]

  c) Write down the mode of the scores.   [1]

15 A different group of students completed another test.

Their marks out of 35 were: 25, 28, 24, 26, 23, 27, 26

  a) Work out the mean of the marks achieved by the students. Show your workings and give your answer to two decimal places.   [2]

  b) Work out the percentage score for the student who achieved the lowest number of marks. Show your workings and give your answer to two significant figures.   [2]

  c) Draw an appropriate graph to represent the marks that each student achieved. Label the axes and provide a suitable title for your graph.   [4]

Social Influence

Where space is not provided, write your answers on a separate piece of paper.

1 In Asch's conformity study, participants were shown a line and asked to identify which of the three comparison lines was the same length. Which of the following did the study aim to investigate? Shade **one** box only. **[1]**

    A The effect of authority figures on obedience ◯

    B The impact of social facilitation on performance ◯

    C The role of group influence on conformity ◯

    D The relationship between personality traits and leadership ◯

2 Describe the influence of group size on conformity. Use an example in your answer. **[3]**

3 Discuss how dispositional factors can affect conforming to a majority. Use an example in your answer. **[6]**

4 Describe and evaluate Asch's line study. In your description, include the method used, the results obtained and a conclusion drawn. **[9]**

5 Milgram's agency theory suggests that obedience to authority is influenced by several social factors. Which of the following is **not** one of the factors highlighted by the theory? Shade **one** box only. **[1]**

    A Agency ◯

    B Authority ◯

    C Task difficulty ◯

    D Proximity ◯

6 Use your knowledge of psychology to evaluate Milgram's agency theory of obedience. **[5]**

7 Briefly outline Adorno's theory of the Authoritarian Personality. **[3]**

8 As part of his Authoritarian Personality theory, Adorno suggested that obedience is influenced by which of the following? Shade **one** box only. **[1]**

    A Genetic factors ◯

    B Cultural norms ◯

    C Childhood experiences ◯

    D Cognitive dissonance ◯

9 Adorno used the F-scale to measure how authoritarian people were. Outline **one** weakness in using a questionnaire. **[2]**

_____

_____

10 Outline **one** difference between using a questionnaire and an interview. **[2]**

_____

_____

11 Piliavin's bystander study focused on which of the following? Shade **one** box only. **[1]**

A   Obedience to authority figures ⬡

B   Factors influencing bystander intervention in emergencies ⬡

C   The impact of group size on conformity ⬡

D   The relationship between personality traits and leadership ⬡

12 Piliavin's study utilised a simulated emergency situation involving which of the following? Shade **one** box only. **[1]**

A   A staged argument between two actors ⬡

B   A fake electrical shock apparatus ⬡

C   A person appearing to be in need of medical assistance ⬡

D   A series of moral dilemmas presented to participants ⬡

13 Explain how social factors (the presence of others and the cost of helping) affect bystander intervention. **[4]**

14 Explain how dispositional factors (similarity to victim and expertise) affect bystander intervention. **[4]**

15 Describe deindividuation, using an example in your answer. **[3]**

16 Identify and explain **two** dispositional factors that influence collective behaviour. **[4]**

Language, Thought and Communication

Where space is not provided, write your answers on a separate piece of paper.

1 According to Piaget's theory of language depends on which of the following? Shade **one** box only. **[1]**

A   Social interactions and imitation ◯

B   Biological factors and innate abilities ◯

C   Thought and cognitive processes ◯

D   Cultural influences and exposure ◯

2 What does the Sapir-Whorf hypothesis suggest? Shade **one** box only. **[1]**

A   Language determines our thoughts and perceptions ◯

B   Language is influenced by cultural norms and values ◯

C   Language is a universal human trait ◯

D   Language acquisition is primarily a biological process ◯

3 Explain the difference between Piaget's and Sapir-Whorf's theories regarding the possible relationship between language and thought. **[4]**

4 Describe how language variation can affect recall of events and recognition of colours. **[4]**

5 A researcher collected data from people speaking different languages around the world. They collected the data via a questionnaire. The following results show the total number of colours they have words for:

People	Colour
Zuni	5
Berinmo	5
Dani	2

What problems would individuals from these cultures encounter when shown a colour chart used in Western societies? **[3]**

6 Other than socially desirable responses, what problems might the researcher have encountered using a questionnaire? **[3]**

7 Describe Von Frisch's bee study. **[4]**

8 Evaluate Von Frisch's bee study. **[4]**

9 Animal communication has a limited number of functions when compared with human communication. Match each function of communication with its description.   **[4]**

A | To attract a mate
B | To mark their area, using urine for example
C | To draw attention to a source of nourishment
D | To make an alarm call as a warning

i) | Food
ii) | Survival
iii) | Reproduction
iv) | Territory

10 Name **one** property of human communication that is not present in animal communication. Use an example in your answer.   **[2]**

....

....

11 A researcher decided to carry out an observation on monkeys in captivity to record their communication with each other. Give **one** category of behaviour that the researcher could observe.   **[1]**

....

12 The researcher was concerned about the reliability of the observation. Explain how this could be assessed and improved.   **[4]**

13 Outline **one** strength and **one** weakness of carrying out an observation.   **[4]**

14 Outline **one** difference between verbal and non-verbal communication. Give an example of each in your answer.   **[4]**

15 Identify **three** functions of eye contact.   **[3]**

16 A researcher wanted to investigate eye movement and whether it affected the flow of conversation. People who happened to be in the cafe were asked if they would participate in a study and if they were free to meet in the psychology lab at a given time. On arrival they were randomly paired with people they had never met and sat at a table. One pair at a time was asked to get to know each other. The researcher covertly observed their interaction in a one-way mirror. The eye movements were recorded. It was found that when a person was finishing speaking they would give a prolonged look to the other person. If they were about to speak, they would break eye contact. It was concluded that eye contact did provide non-verbal cues for conversing with someone else.

a) Which sampling method was used for this study?   **[1]**

....

b) Referring to the study above, how did they use eye contact to regulate the flow of the conversation? **[4]**

c) How could the people be randomly paired? **[2]**

....

....

d) What is a covert observation? **[2]**

....

....

e) Explain an ethical issue that would need to be addressed with a covert observation. **[2]**

....

....

f) With reference to one function of eye contact, what conclusions could be reached in this study (apart from the one stated)? **[3]**

17 What is postural echo? **[2]**

....

....

18 Outline **one** difference between closed posture and open posture. **[2]**

....

....

19 How could cultural norms affect touch as a form of body language? **[2]**

....

....

20 Using the table below, briefly describe how each of the factors affects personal space. **[6]**

Factor affecting personal space	Description
Culture	
Status	
Gender	

21 Describe Darwin's evolutionary theory of non-verbal communication. **[4]**

22 Explain what evidence there is to suggest that non-verbal behaviour is innate. **[4]**

23 Describe and evaluate Yuki's study of emoticons. **[6]**

Brain and Neuropsychology

Where space is not provided, write your answers on a separate piece of paper.

1 The human nervous system is divided into which main divisions? Shade **one** box only. **[2]**

   A Central and somatic ⬜

   B Peripheral and autonomic ⬜

   C Somatic and autonomic ⬜

   D Central and peripheral ⬜

2 The central nervous system consists of which of the following? Shade **one** box only. **[1]**

   A The brain and spinal cord ⬜

   B Nerves and ganglia ⬜

   C Sensory receptors and effectors ⬜

   D Sympathetic and parasympathetic systems ⬜

3 The peripheral nervous system is further divided into which of the following? Shade **one** box only. **[2]**

   A Sensory and motor divisions ⬜

   B Somatic and autonomic divisions ⬜

   C Sympathetic and parasympathetic divisions ⬜

   D Cerebral cortex and limbic system ⬜

4 What does the somatic division of the peripheral nervous system control? Shade **one** box only. **[1]**

   A Involuntary bodily functions ⬜

   B Conscious movements and sensory perception ⬜

   C Fight-or-flight responses ⬜

   D Internal organs and glands ⬜

5 The autonomic division of the peripheral nervous system regulates which of the following? Shade **one** box only. **[1]**

A Voluntary muscle movements ◯

B Somatic reflexes and reactions ◯

C Heart rate, digestion and glandular activity ◯

D Sensory processing and perception ◯

6 Outline **one** difference between the somatic nervous system and the autonomic nervous system. **[2]**

_____

_____

7 Describe the fight or flight response. **[5]**

8 What is adrenaline? **[1]**

_____

9 Describe the James-Lange theory of emotion. **[4]**

10 What are sensory neurons responsible for? Shade **one** box only. **[1]**

A Transmitting signals from the brain to the body ◯

B Controlling voluntary muscle movements ◯

C Receiving and transmitting sensory information ◯

D Initiating and regulating immune responses ◯

11 What are motor neurons responsible for? Shade **one** box only. **[1]**

A Transmitting signals from the brain to the body ◯

B Controlling involuntary muscle contractions ◯

C Receiving and transmitting sensory information ◯

D Initiating and regulating immune responses ◯

12 Describe the process of synaptic transmission. **[5]**

13 What did Hebb suggest about learning and neuronal growth? **[4]**

14 Describe the **four** lobes of the brain and the function of each. **[6]**

Brain and Neuropsychology

15 Label the areas of the brain that are responsible for motor, somatosensory, visual, auditory and language skills. **[6]**

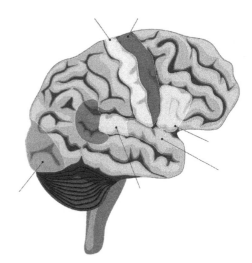

16 What is cognitive neuroscience? **[3]**

17 Complete **Table 1**. **[5]**

Table 1.

	fMRI	PET	CT
How it works	Measures changes in blood flow		Produces X-ray images
What it does		Measures brain activity	Provides detailed structural images
Resolution	High		High
Exposure to radiation	No		

18 Describe Tulving's 'gold' memory study. **[4]**

19 Describe how neurological damage such as stroke or injury can affect motor abilities and behaviour. **[4]**

Psychological Problems

Where space is not provided, write your answers on a separate piece of paper.

1 How has the incidence of mental health problems changed over time? [2]

....

....

2 Give **one** reason why this might be the case. [2]

....

....

3 How does culture affect the perception of mental health problems? [2]

....

....

4 Describe **two** characteristics of good mental health. [2]

....

....

5 Describe how the stigma of mental health problems has been reduced. [2]

....

....

6 A researcher wanted to find out if there was a relationship between people coping with stressful life events and their incidence of depression. Stressful life events were measured via a self-report questionnaire (the Social Readjustment Rating Scale (SRRS)) and the extent of someone's depression was also measured via self-report using Beck's Depression Inventory (BDI).

Scores of both were collected.

a) One factor that could influence life events is modern living. Identify a potential factor of modern living. [1]

....

b) The study above suggests that stressful life events and depression could be correlated. If both scores are high on the two questionnaires, what we could assume about depression? [2]

....

....

c) The researcher is collecting quantitative data. How could the researcher collect qualitative data in this study? [3]

Psychological Problems

The results for the study are shown in **Table 1**.

Table 1.

Participant	1	2	3	4	5
SRRS score	12	14	12	16	17
BDI score	9	10	18	11	12

d) Draw a scatter graph of the data. Include a title and label both axes.   **[4]**

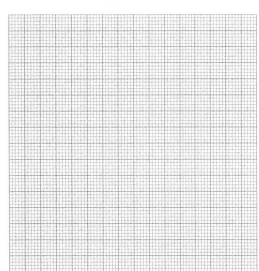

7 Describe **one** difference between unipolar and bipolar depression.   **[2]**

_____

_____

8 Classification systems for mental health problems have been in place for over a hundred years. Give **one** reason why they are frequently updated.   **[2]**

_____

_____

9 Briefly discuss a strength of using the International Classification of Diseases (ICD) in diagnosing unipolar depression.   **[3]**

10 Unipolar depression is characterised by which of the following? Shade **one** box only.   **[1]**

A Periods of extreme mood swings   ○

B Fluctuating episodes of depression and mania   ○

C Persistent feelings of sadness and loss of interest   ○

D Symptoms of anxiety and panic attacks   ○

11 Which **one** of the following are symptoms of bipolar depression? Shade **one** box only.   **[1]**

A   Excessive happiness and euphoria   ◯

B   Chronic fatigue and low energy levels   ◯

C   Hallucinations and delusions   ◯

D   Mania and depression   ◯

12 According to the biological explanation of depression, which neurotransmitter is commonly implicated? Shade **one** box only.   **[1]**

A   Serotonin   ◯

B   Acetylcholine   ◯

C   Endorphins   ◯

D   Histamine   ◯

13 Describe **one** strength and **one** weakness of the biological explanation of depression.   **[4]**

14 According to the cognitive explanation of depression, individuals with depression tend to do which of the following? Shade **one** box only.   **[1]**

A   Have overly positive thoughts and beliefs   ◯

B   Focus on positive aspects of their lives   ◯

C   Engage in negative thinking patterns   ◯

D   Have accurate perceptions of reality   ◯

15 Describe **one** strength and **one** weakness of the psychological explanation of depression.   **[4]**

16 There are different interventions for the treatment of depression, one is regarded as reductionist and the other is regarded as more holistic. Describe and evaluate both the interventions using examples in your answer.   **[9]**

17 Outline the difference between addiction and substance abuse.   **[2]**

---

18   Cary has been prescribed painkillers for a bad back that she sustained in an accident. She started off with one tablet three time a day but now takes two tablets three times a day as she said she 'got used to the pills' and that 'they no longer numbed the pain'.

Is Cary showing signs of substance dependence or misuse? Explain your answer.   **[4]**

Psychological Problems

19 The ICD criteria for addiction include which of the following? Shade **one** box only.   [1]

A   Withdrawal symptoms   ◯

B   Priority given to substance   ◯

C   Strong desire to use   ◯

D   All of the above   ◯

20 What is meant by genetic vulnerability to addiction?   [2]

....

....

21 How have researchers investigated a genetic explanation of addiction?   [3]

22 This method of investigation that is influenced by nature has its problems.
Identify **one** problem with the method of investigation.   [2]

....

....

23 Describe how Kaij investigated alcohol abuse.   [4]

24 What conclusions can be made from Kaij's findings?   [2]

....

....

25 Ashley has been drinking alcohol on a regular basis since she started work. Her work colleagues who are of a similar age to Ashley, all go for drinks after work so she has been joining them. She has noticed that her wages don't last as long as they did and she has started to borrow money so she can continue to go out after work. Her friends who she went to school with have complained that she no longer prioritises them over her new friends.

What aspects of Ashley's behaviour suggest she may be developing a dependence on alcohol?   [3]

26 Describe how a psychological explanation would explain Ashley's behaviour.   [4]

Collins

GCSE Psychology
Paper 1: Cognition and Behaviour

Time allowed: 1 hour 45 minutes

The maximum mark for this paper is 100

Materials

> **For this paper you may have:**
>
> - a calculator.

Instructions

- Use black ink or black ball-point pen.
- Answer **all** questions. You must answer the questions in the spaces provided.
- Do all rough work in this book.

Information

- The marks for questions are shown in brackets.
- Questions should be answered in continuous prose. You will be assessed on your ability to:
  - use good English
  - organise information clearly
  - use specialist vocabulary where appropriate.

Name: ....

Practice Exam Paper 1

Section A
Memory

Answer all questions in the spaces provided.

---

0 1 James goes to the supermarket without writing a list. Once there, he gets mixed up with the fruit and vegetables that he needed to purchase. If James is accessing his long-term memory for the information, how has this been encoded? Shade **one** box only. **[1 mark]**

A Visually ◯

B Semantically ◯

C Acoustically ◯

D Olfactory ◯

0 2 Bartlett's War of the Ghosts study investigated reconstructive memory. What is meant by 'reconstructive memory'? **[2 marks]**

---

0 3 Bartlett's study asked participants to retell a story several times. The procedure was not well controlled. Identify **one** problem with having a lack of control over the procedures when carrying out research. **[2 marks]**

---

0 4 Stella is sporty and participates in various team sports for her college. However, sometimes her teammates get frustrated with her when she seems to ignore the court markings and the rules for netball after she has played basketball.

0 4 · 1 Name the factor that is affecting Stella's accuracy of memory. **[1 mark]**

---

0 4 . 2 Using your knowledge of this factor, explain why Stella's teammates get frustrated with her.

[4 marks]

---

0 5 A group of year 10 students believe that if they sit their end-of-year mocks in their classrooms they will perform better. They lobby fellow pupils who agree. They then present a proposal to the school to be allowed to sit exams in their classroom rather than the hall.

0 5 . 1 Using your knowledge of the accuracy of memory, explain why the students are convinced that they will perform better in the exams if they are allowed to sit them in their classes.

Briefly evaluate this explanation.

[9 marks]

---

0 5 . 2 Outline the differences between episodic, semantic and procedural memories. Use examples in your answer. **[6 marks]**

Section B
Perception
Answer **all** questions in the spaces provided.

---

0 6 Which **one** of the following is not an explanation of a misinterpreted depth cue?
Shade **one** box only.   **[1 mark]**

A The Ponzo illusion   ◯

B The Muller-Lyer illusion   ◯

C Rubin's vase   ◯

D The Ames Room   ◯

0 7 Identify **one** monocular depth cue.   **[1 mark]**

....

0 8 · 1 Explain what is meant by size constancy. Include an example.   **[3 marks]**

....

....

....

....

0 8 · 2 Identify **one** binocular depth cue and explain how it works.   **[4 marks]**

....

....

....

....

....

0 9 Briefly evaluate Bruner and Minturn's study of perceptual set. **[4 marks]**

_____

_____

_____

_____

1 0 Explain how Gregory's constructivist theory of perception is influenced by nurture. **[4 marks]**

_____

_____

_____

_____

1 1 · 1 Describe Gibson's direct theory of visual perception. **[4 marks]**

_____

_____

_____

_____

1 1 · 2 Explain how Gibson's theory of perception is influenced by nature, using research evidence. **[4 marks]**

_____

_____

_____

_____

Section C
Development
Answer all questions in the spaces provided.

---

1 2 · 1 Which **one** of the following best describes the brain stem?
Shade **one** box only. **[1 mark]**

A Located deep inside the brain ⬡

B Most highly developed part of the brain at birth ⬡

C The last part of the brain to reach maturity ⬡

D Where thinking takes place ⬡

1 2 · 2 Which **one** of the following best describes the function of the cerebellum?
Shade **one** box only. **[1 mark]**

A Processes auditory information ⬡

B Controls automatic functions ⬡

C Processes visual information ⬡

D Co-ordinates movement and balance ⬡

1 3 · 1 Which **one** of the following best describes the role of nurture in
early brain development? Shade **one** box only. **[1 mark]**

A The way our brain forms is inherited ⬡

B The way our brain forms depends on our environment ⬡

C Our brain's development relies on our genes and environment ⬡

Practice Exam Paper 1

1 3 · 2 Which **one** of the following best describes the role of nature in early brain development? Shade **one** box only. **[1 mark]**

    A The way our brain forms is inherited ◯

    B The way our brain forms depends on our environment ◯

    C Our brain's development relies on our genes and environment ◯

1 3 · 3 What did Piaget mean by 'egocentricism'? **[2 marks]**

....

....

1 4 Byron's two children are Kane who is three and Tulula who is four. When playing hide and seek, Kane hides on the sofa under cushions so is clearly visible. Tulula hides in places where she is unseen. Kane gets upset as he cannot work out why he cannot find Tulula but she finds him easily.

1 4 · 1 Name the stage of cognitive development that Kane is in. **[1 mark]**

....

1 4 · 2 Explain how Tulula is showing a reduction in egocentrism. **[3 marks]**

....

....

....

....

1 5 · 1 You are interested in Piaget's theory of egocentrism. Using three-year-old children in their nursery playground, design an observation to see if they display egocentrism. You need to include:

- What type of observation and why

- At least **two** examples of behaviour you could observe

- One ethical issue that you would need to address and how you could deal with it. **[6 marks]**

1 5 · 2 Briefly outline a fixed mindset. **[2 marks]**

Jamal, Mina and Carlos were revising. Carlos said he cannot revise for exams and would prefer to be completing his media work, making videos and designing magazine covers. Mina has lots of mind maps and diagrams to aid her revision. Jamal continuously writes notes and even rewrites them.

`1 5`·`3` Describe and explain the learning styles each is displaying. **[6 marks]**

....

....

....

....

....

....

....

....

....

....

`1 5`·`4` Which **one** of the following is a criticism of learning styles, according Willingham? Shade **one** box only. **[1 mark]**

A Learning styles are scientific ☐

B Learning styles show how children learn ☐

C Learning styles are unscientific ☐

Section D
Research methods
Answer all questions in the spaces provided.

---

1 6 Serena is carrying out research on people's views of UFOs. She decided to interview each participant who responded to her advert in an air and space magazine. Serena used a structured interview.

1 6 · 1 Some of the participants may have felt embarrassed if they agreed with the existence of UFOs. This would be an ethical issue. Describe this ethical issue and suggest **one** way Serena could deal with it.   **[4 marks]**

....

....

....

....

1 6 · 2 Explain **one** weakness of using a structured interview.   **[2 marks]**

....

....

Participants who indicated that they believed in UFOs were asked back for a further interview. This time Serena used an unstructured interview.

1 7 · 1 Name the type of data that Serena would gather using an unstructured interview.   **[1 mark]**

....

1 7 · 2 Explain the difference between an unstructured and a structured interview.   **[4 marks]**

Another researcher analysed the data Serena collected. They had noticed in the interviews that people who held a strong belief in the existence of UFOs were very confident. The second researcher decided to carry out a correlation between the participant's confidence and their belief in UFOs. They predicted that the more confident they were, the stronger their belief would be.

1 7 · 3 Write a suitable hypothesis for this correlation.   **[2 marks]**

1 7 · 4 Name the type of correlation that will be found if the researcher's prediction is true.   **[1 mark]**

1 7 · 5 What is the strength of using a correlation for this research?   **[3 marks]**

1 8 · 1 Using the graph paper, sketch a scatter diagram to show the results in **Table 1**.
Provide a suitable title and labels for your diagram. **[4 marks]**

Table 1.

Participant	Confidence/10	Beliefs/10
1	3	7
2	5	8
3	8	10
4	9	9
5	3	6
6	5	7
7	4	4
8	10	8
9	7	9
10	6	9

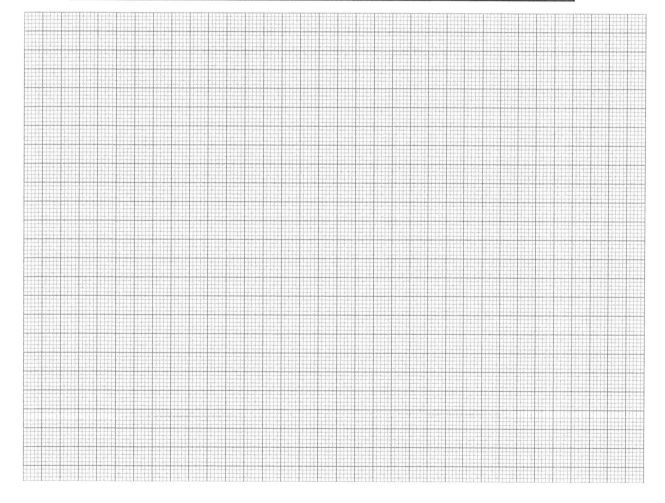

1 8 · 2 Identify the mode for the confidence ratings. **[1 mark]**

_____

1 8 · 3 Identify the mode for the beliefs rating. **[1 mark]**

_____

1 8 · 4 The median for the confidence was 5.5 and the mean was 6. What type of distribution is shown in the confidence ratings? Shade **one** box only. **[1 mark]**

A Normal ◯

B Negative ◯

C Positive ◯

1 8 · 5 The correlation was carried out by another researcher using the original data collected by Serena. What would this data be called? Shade **one** box only. **[1 mark]**

A Secondary ◯

B Primary ◯

C Normal ◯

Collins

GCSE Psychology
Paper 2: Social Context and Behaviour

Time allowed: 1 hour 45 minutes

The maximum mark for this paper is 100

Materials

For this paper you may have:

- a calculator.

Instructions

- Use black ink or black ball-point pen.
- Answer all questions. You must answer the questions in the spaces provided.
- Do all rough work in this book.

Information

- The marks for questions are shown in brackets.
- Questions should be answered in continuous prose. You will be assessed on your ability to:
  - use good English
  - organise information clearly
  - use specialist vocabulary where appropriate.

Name: ....

Practice Exam Paper 2

Section A
Social Influence

Answer all questions in the spaces provided.

0 1 In Asch's study of conformity the genuine participant would usually be one of the last because of which of the following? Shade **one** box only. **[1 mark]**

    A It would increase the chances of demand characteristics ◯

    B It was an unambiguous situation so participants did not need to see how to behave, which would show conformity ◯

    C They would hear a minority of answers ◯

    D It was an ambiguous situation so participants needed to see how to behave, which would show conformity. ◯

0 2 Tom and Lilah were having a conversation about their psychology lessons. Lilah told Tom that he only answers questions when at least three others have already answered, so he conforms to their answers. Tom disputes this and accuses Lilah of the same. Lilah says she only ever conforms to other people's answers for guidance when the question is challenging.

0 2 · 1 Explain using social factors why Lilah thinks that Tom conforms during their lessons. **[2 marks]**

....

....

0 2 · 2 Explain using task difficulty why Lilah claims to only conform if the question is difficult. Use research evidence in your answer. **[3 marks]**

....

....

....

`0 3`·`1` In Milgram's study, what percentage of participants went to 300 volts? **[1 mark]**

....

....

`0 3`·`2` Compare Milgram's explanation of obedience with Adorno's explanation of obedience. **[4 marks]**

....

....

....

....

....

`0 4`·`1` Describe the **two** independent variables in Piliavin's subway study and explain how they were clearly defined. **[4 marks]**

....

....

....

....

`0 4`·`2` How did the Piliavin study collect the data? **[1 mark]**

....

`0 4`·`3` Explain **one** weakness of collecting the data for this study in this way. **[2 marks]**

....

....

0 5 Researchers carried out an observation looking at helping behaviour. They observed whether wearing a uniform influenced behaviour. Participants were told they were taking part in a study of helping others. They were given either a nurse's uniform or a football top and shorts or they remained in their own clothes. They then completed a computer simulation where different scenarios were shown where people needed help such as when falling over. They had to indicate whether they would help or not. For each scenario they were told if they helped it could come at personal cost to them, such as missing a job interview because they would be late.

Table 1.

Number of helping scenarios	People dressed as a nurse helping	People in football kit helping	Own clothes helping
12	8	3	5

0 5 · 1 Identify and describe the social factor that could explain the behaviour in **Table 1**. [2 marks]

0 5 · 2 Using research, evaluate how social factors affect collective behaviour. [5 marks]

Section B
Language, thought and communication
Answer all questions in the spaces provided.

---

0 6 Outline how language affects the recall of events and colour recognition in different cultures. **[4 marks]**

....

....

....

....

0 7 Describe **two** ethical issues that could arise when carrying out research into personal space. **[4 marks]**

....

....

....

....

0 8 Which behaviours are functions of animal behaviour and which behaviours are functions of human behaviour? Write **A** or **B** in the boxes.

A = Animal, B = Human **[4 marks]**

Planning ahead	
Leave pheromones	
Use communication for specific events	
Advertise fitness	

0 9 Which **one** of the following is an example that does not show innate non-verbal communication? Shade **one** box only. **[1 mark]**

A Neonates using non-verbal behaviours such as smiling ⬜

B Babies show a disgusted facial expression when given something sour ⬜

C Children born blind have been found to show facial expressions, such as surprise ⬜

D People from contact cultures prefer a small personal space whereas people from non-contact cultures prefer a larger one. ⬜

1 0 Piaget said children can only understand words when they are cognitively ready. Sapir & Whorf would suggest the opposite – that language comes before thought. Use your knowledge of both Piaget and Sapir & Whorf to discuss the way language develops. **[9 marks]**

....

....

....

....

....

....

....

....

....

....

1 | 1 | Briefly describe Yuki's study of emoticons.   **[3 marks]**

....

....

....

....

Section C
Brain and neuropsychology

Answer **all** questions in the spaces provided.

| 1 | 2 | Complete boxes A, B, C and D.

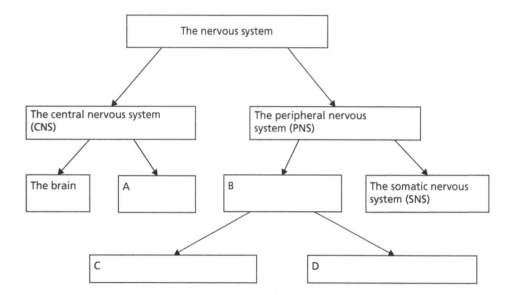

[4 marks]

| 1 | 3 | Which **one** of the following is false regarding the fight or flight response? Shade **one** box only.
[1 mark]

A The hormone adrenaline is released from the adrenal glands ◯

B The hypothalamus detects a stressor (a threat) ◯

C Adrenaline causes the heartrate to slow down ◯

D When the threat is over, saliva is produced again ◯

1 4 A patient who suffered a brain injury and then had some memory problems, attended the hospital. The doctor discussed an appropriate scan to find out the extent of the damage.

1 4 · 1 Identify three scans the doctor could discuss with the patient. **[3 marks]**

....

....

....

....

1 4 · 2 Name the scan that would be able to detect the area of the brain being used whilst carrying out a memory task, without using radiation. **[1 mark]**

....

....

1 4 · 3 Evaluate the scanning technique that does not use radiation. **[4 marks]**

....

....

....

....

....

1 5 Evaluate Hebb's theory of learning and neuronal growth. **[4 marks]**

....

....

....

....

....

....

1 6 Name the hemisphere of the brain where we usually find the language areas. **[1 mark]**

1 7 Name the area of the brain that contains the somatosensory area. **[1 mark]**

1 8 What is cognitive neuroscience? How has it helped us to understand neurological damage? **[6 marks]**

Section D
Psychological problems
Answer **all** questions in the spaces provided.

---

1 9 Which **two** of the following are often seen in people with unipolar depression?
Shade **two** boxes. **[2 marks]**

A Appetite changes (loss or increase) ◯

B Being happier in usual activities ◯

C Disruption of sleep pattern (sleeping more or less) ◯

D Greater self-confidence and esteem ◯

2 0 Explain how significant mental health problems can affect the individual. **[6 marks]**

2 1 Out-patients attending a clinic for treatment for their depression were asked to take part in research. The participants were the ones who happened to be there on that day and who agreed to take part. The study consisted of them giving a score of their symptoms on that day. They were then asked if they would repeat the questionnaire after six months. The first set of data received from the questionnaires (out of ten for severity of symptoms) gave the following scores:

5, 6, 7, 8, 8, 8, 9, 9, 10, 10

2 1 . 1 Which sampling method was used in this study? Justify your answer.   **[2 marks]**

_____

_____

2 1 . 2 Calculate the median rating of severity of symptoms. Show your workings. **[2 marks]**

_____

_____

2 1 . 3 After six months the same participants filled in the same questionnaire giving the following scores: 3, 3, 3, 3, 6, 6, 6, 7, 7, 7

The median rating in the follow-up study was 6. Explain what the results suggest about the effectiveness of the treatment the patients were receiving, referring to the median scores.   **[4 marks]**

_____

_____

_____

_____

_____

_____

2 1 · 4 Identify and evaluate **one** therapy the patients could have been given in this study. [5 marks]

_____

_____

_____

_____

_____

2 2 Outline peer influence as a psychological explanation of addiction. [4 marks]

_____

_____

_____

_____

_____

Notes

GCSE Psychology Workbook

Answers

1. Alina: semantic [1]; George: visual [1]
2. **Encoding:** the process of acquiring, processing and organising incoming information in a way that allows it to be stored and later retrieved from memory. [2]
   Storage: the phase of memory where information that has been encoded is retained and maintained over time. [2]
   Retrieval: the process of accessing and recalling stored information from memory. It involves locating and bringing back the stored information to conscious awareness. [2]
3. A and B should be shaded. [2]
4. Storage can be in short-term memory, held for a short time up to 30 seconds. Storage can be in long-term memory for up to a lifetime. [2]
5. Bobby uses cued recall to remember the names of the football teams, such as his friend giving him the first letter to help him. Anil uses recognition to help him remember the names of the teams – once he is shown a list of all the team names, he can recognise the ones in their league. Nick doesn't need help, he can free recall the names of the football teams without any aid. [6]
6. Research supporting semantic memory as a separate type of memory comes from the Clive Wearing case study. Clive had damage to his hippocampus but could still remember facts and retained the ability to speak and understand language (semantic memory). Clive Wearing's case also supports the notion that we have a separate memory of procedural information. For example, Clive retained the ability to play the piano, even after his brain damage (a type of procedural memory). However, he was unable to retain his episodic memory (the ability to recall episodes in your life). He could not remember much of his life prior to his illness and this demonstrates that episodic memory is in a different part of the brain to semantic and procedural memory. [5]
7. According to the MSM, memory is divided into three main stores:
   Sensory Memory (SM): holds incoming sensory information from the environment for a very brief period. It codes information via the five senses. SM allows for a brief retention of sensory stimuli, giving us a continuous perception of the world. If information is paid attention to it will transfer to the STM. **Short-term Memory (STM):** has a limited capacity of 5-9 items and duration of up to 30 seconds without rehearsal. Without rehearsal or further processing, information in STM is likely to be forgotten. It codes information acoustically. Rehearsal will transfer information to LTM. **Long-term Memory (LTM):** has a vast capacity and stores information for a relatively longer duration, from minutes to a lifetime. LTM is believed to have an unlimited capacity, although retrieval of information from LTM can vary in terms of accessibility. It codes information semantically. [6]
8. One strength of the model is it shows us that we have separate stores for short-term and long-term memories. Evidence supports this idea. [2]
9. The duration of STM is up to 30 seconds.
10. a) Archie [1]
    b) primacy and recency effect. [1]
11. Short term memory only holds information for up to 30 seconds [1], whereas long term memory can store information permanently, potentially a lifetime. [1]
12. Murdock's study supports the MSM as participants could recall the first words in the list, because they would have been rehearsed and transferred to LTM. The words at the end were recalled easily as they were the most recent and still in the short-term memory. [4]
13. D and E should be shaded. [2]
14. The focus on the meaning of events rather than the details. For example, describing the way people try to make sense of new information, by using past information to make sense of it, such as in the War of the Ghosts study. [2]
15. Reconstructive memory is when we fill in any gaps in our memories using our existing schemas so we can make sense of things. For example, in the Bartlett study, participants had no idea in places what the story was about so they reconstructed the story to retell it using their own schemas based on experience and culture. [3]
16. Participants tended to omit or simplify details of the story that were unfamiliar or culturally inconsistent with their own background. They unconsciously filled in gaps with information that was more familiar and coherent with their own schemas. The story became more familiar and aligned with their own cultural norms and expectations and lost its original cultural context, such as using 'boats' rather than 'canoes'. [3]
17. a) Lab experiment [1]
    b) A weakness of a lab experiment is that they can have low validity as the set-up doesn't really reflect a real-life situation. [2]
18. False memories are memories about an event that did not happen but the person feels that it did. For example, in a study by Loftus where participants were given four short stories about their childhood, three were true and one wasn't. The participants had to read each story and write down afterwards what they remembered. Six of the participants recalled the false story as being true. [3]
19. **The procedure:** Participants could be gathered using an opportunity sample – people who were there at the time for a lesson. You could give the participants a topic to revise for thirty minutes, followed by a test. Both revision and the test take place in the same classroom. On a different day, the same group could be given a different topic of equal difficulty to revise in the psychology room but sit the test in a different classroom. The test would get a score out of twenty.
    Hypothesis: Participants who revise and sit the psychology test in the same room will get a higher score out of twenty compared to if they revise in one classroom and sit the test in a different room.
    Expected results: In line with context affecting the accuracy of memory, the results should show that the students' scores are higher when they sat the test in the same room as they revised. Context acts as a cue for recall. This would be in line with research, such as Godden and Baddeley, who found when the context of learning either underwater or at a beach was different to recall, participants performed worse. [6]

1. Sensation refers to the process of detecting and receiving sensory information from the environment through our sensory organs such as eyes, ears, mouth, nose and skin. In order for us to make sense of the information, our brain needs to interpret these sensations and this is what perception is. Perception is the process of interpreting and making sense of the sensory information received through sensation. It involves the organisation, identification, and interpretation of sensory inputs by the brain. [4]
2. Monocular depth cues are visual cues that provide information about depth and distance using only one eye. These cues help us perceive depth and three-dimensional space, even when we view the world with just a single eye. [2]

3. B and D should be shaded. **[2]**
4. Binocular depth cues are visual cues that rely on the use of both eyes to perceive depth and three-dimensional space. These cues take advantage of the slight differences in the images received by each eye to create a sense of depth perception. **[2]**

5.
[1]

6. Psychologists would explain the Ponzo illusion based on our perception of depth and distance. Our brain uses various depth cues, such as linear perspective and size-distance relationship, to judge the relative size and distance of objects. In the Ponzo illusion, the converging lines create the impression of depth, so the depth cue is misinterpreted, with the top line appearing further away and the bottom line appearing closer. **[3]**

7. a)
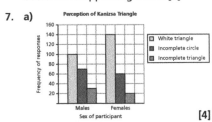
[4]

b) 200 ÷ 20 = 10
220 ÷ 20 = 11 so ratio is 10:11 **[2]**
c) (140/220) × 100 = 0.6364 × 100 = 63.64% to three significant figures = 63.6 **[2]**
d) D

8. Perceptual set refers to a predisposition or readiness to perceive certain stimuli or interpret sensory information in a particular way. It is influenced by our prior experiences, expectations, beliefs, and cultural factors. We 'see' what we want to see. **[2]**

9. Perceptual set can be affected by culture. Culture refers to the shared beliefs, values, norms and practices of a particular group or society. It influences the way individuals perceive and interpret the world around them. What we are familiar with influences our interpretation of things. **[2]**

10. Researchers would expect the vegetarians to take longer to complete the word search in condition two (the meat-related one). This is because emotion can affect perceptual set and, in this case, the vegetarians may have blocked out the words to do with meat as they may have found them threatening or anxiety-inducing. **[3]**

11. Findings may be unreliable because on some days people may be more likely to notice emotional stimuli and on other days less likely to notice. Therefore depending on the person's mood on a particular day could affect the findings. **[2]**

12. Gilchrist and Nesberg's study has support from other researchers, showing it has validity. Other studies found motivation influenced behaviour, such as being hungry influences our perception and interpretation of pictures. The Gilchrist and Nesberg study could have had ethical issues as preventing people from eating could be problematic. People went without food for twenty hours which could affect some participants. The study also is low in validity as they didn't use real food to show to participants, only pictures, so may not be generalisable to real-life situations. **[4]**

13. 24 participants were split into two groups where half were shown some letters with an ambiguous figure in the middle, a B that was broken that could read as 13 or B. The other half were shown some numbers with the same ambiguous figure in the middle. Bruner and Minturn found the participants in the number group mostly drew 13. The group who saw letters mainly drew a B. The researchers concluded that expectation affects perception. **[6]**

14. The name of the perceptual set is emotion. This is similar to research carried out where participants had to look at displayed words – some were taboo whilst others were neutral. They measured their skin conductance as a sign of anxiety. The taboo words took longer for the participants to say out loud and their skin conductance increased showing they were more anxious. **[4]**

15. Because it was collected solely for the purpose of this study. It wasn't collected by someone else. **[2]**

<hr>
Pages 11–14 **Development**

1. C
2. Processes in the body that are outside of our conscious control, such as our heart beating. We do not have to think about it, it does it automatically. **[3]**
3. B
4. The influence on our behaviour that is external. Anything outside of the body, such as a person's environment, could play a role in the nurturing of a person and ultimately affect their behaviour. **[2]**
5. Infection can be considered nurture that could affect a growing brain. For example, pregnant women, in the first twenty weeks, need to keep away from others who have German measles

because they could put the baby at risk of brain damage. **[1]**
6. 87 − 69 = 18
18/87 = 0.20689655 × 100 = 20.68 to two significant figures = 21 **[3]**
7. Opportunity sample as she asked people who were attending the clinic who were present and available at the time. **[2]**
8. Our internal processes that influence our behaviour, through our genes from our parents and ancestors. **[2]**
9. a) A-brain stem, B-cerebral cortex, C-cerebellum, D-Thalamus

b)		
Autonomic functions such as breathing and heartbeat	A
Precise physical movement/ coordinates actions	C
Cognition/thinking/ perception/memory processes	B
Some sensory processing/ relaying signals to the cerebral cortex	D

[4]

10. Assimilation is the process by which individuals incorporate new information or experiences into their existing cognitive structures or schemas. According to Piaget, children actively engage with the world around them, seeking to make sense of new experiences by relating them to their existing knowledge. Accommodation is the process by which children modify their existing cognitive structures or schemas in response to new information or experiences that cannot be easily assimilated. When children encounter new information or experiences that do not fit into their existing schemas, they undergo accommodation. **[4]**

11. Seb is showing accommodation as his existing schema was that the teacher was nice and that Keshav must be wrong. However, when Seb encountered the same experience that did not fit into his schema of the teacher (and therefore this new experience does not fit his schema), he has undergone accommodation and now his schema has been modified. **[4]**

12. a) Maya is the youngest. **[1]**
b) Around the age of 11 **[1]**
c) Pre-operational **[1]**
13. C
14. Children develop at different rates at some of the stages. For example, in the naughty teddy study, some children at the pre-operational stage, could conserve. Therefore showing a weakness of Piaget's stages as being too rigid. Some children will do things at a different pace. A second weakness is that his research was on European children and could be culturally biased as the age at which the stages are reached can vary between cultures. **[5]**

15. When children can only see things from their own viewpoint and no-one else's. This applies to both physical objects and other's points of view. [2]

16. Piaget presented children with a model containing three small mountains with different characteristics, such as varying heights, shapes and details. Each mountain could be viewed from different angles. The child was seated on one side of the model and shown pictures depicting what each mountain would look like from the perspective of a doll positioned on the other side of the model. The task required the child to choose a picture that accurately represented what the doll would see when looking at the mountains from its position. Piaget found that young children, particularly those in the pre-operational stage (around 2 to 7 years old), consistently chose the picture that matched their own perspective rather than the doll's perspective. [3]

17. 30 children between the ages of three and a half and five years were shown a model comprising two intersecting walls, a "boy" doll and a "policeman" doll. The policeman doll was put in various positions and the children were asked to hide the boy doll from the policeman. A second policeman doll was then introduced, and both dolls were placed at the end of the walls. The child was asked to hide the boy from both policemen; the children now had to take account of two different points of view. 90% were able to put the boy doll where the two policemen could not see it. A more complex situation was introduced with more walls and a third policeman. 90% of four-year-olds were successful. The three-year-olds had more difficulty. This study showed that by age four children have lost their egocentrism because they are able to take the view of another. This study used a lab experiment and so validity was low. The task did not reflect what the children would do in real life. This means we cannot generalise findings to a real-life situation. [9]

18.
Stage	Age
Sensorimotor	0-2 years
Pre-operational	2-7 years
Concrete operational	8-11 years
Formal operational	11+
[4]

19. The sensorimotor stage is the first stage of cognitive development which occurs from birth to approximately two years of age. During this stage, infants and young children learn about the world primarily through their senses and actions. The main characteristics of the sensorimotor stage include object permanence / constancy – where infants gradually develop the understanding that objects continue to exist even when they are out of sight. Development of motor skills occurs where infants explore, learn to grasp objects, crawl, walk and develop other motor skills. The pre-operational stage is the second stage. It typically occurs between the ages of two and seven years. During this stage, children become more capable of symbolic thinking and representation and engage in pretend play and make-believe scenarios. They use objects symbolically and create imaginary situations. Children in this stage tend to have difficulty understanding or considering the perspectives of others. They view the world primarily from their own point of view. [4]

20. Piaget has played a role in education through suggesting there is a stage of cognitive development when children are biologically ready to learn certain things and not before. Activities need to be age-appropriate for learning to take place. Piaget also believed that children learn through discovery rather than by rote, so they play a part alongside the teacher who stimulates the children through activities. These should be suitably challenging. Piaget acknowledged children progress through the stages of development at different rates so activities need to reflect this. This introduced the idea of smaller group activities occurring in the same classroom. Finally, Piaget suggested that, for the different stages of development, there should be a suitable environment in which the stage would be reflected. For example, in the pre-operational stage opportunities for role play should be offered. [4]

21. One weakness of Piaget's theory is that children develop at different rates but according to Piaget there is a set time frame in which development occurs. A second weakness is that his research could be culturally bias as it was carried out on European children. Non-European children could develop at different rates and his research does not acknowledge this fact. [4]

22. A belief that innate abilities are responsible for any achievements. Extra work and trying harder to achieve something is pointless, you won't be able to achieve it, because of the fixed innate abilities you have. If people with a fixed mindset fail at something, they will give up as they think it's pointless. [2]

23. A growth mindset is the opposite of a fixed one. People believe that if they work harder at something, they will experience an improved outcome. They believe that ability can be developed and failure is not an option and they will work harder to achieve. [2]

24. Darragh has a fixed mindset – he believes missing school isn't a problem because he isn't very able and therefore school makes no difference to his abilities. Adam has a growth mindset – he doesn't like missing school as he knows he benefits from being there to improve his abilities. [2]

25. Praise could benefit Darragh as it could increase his motivation to try and work harder and this may improve his abilities. This could improve his self-efficacy: his belief in himself that maybe he could do better if he tried. It could be a motivating force that he needs. Adam already has a positive self-efficacy as he believes he could improve through hard work. This in turn increases his motivation to continue to try and improve. Praise could further Adam's self-efficacy as it would give him feelings of reward which again could motivate him. [6]

26.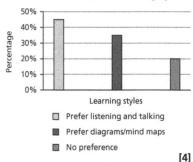

Students preferred learning styles

- ☐ Prefer listening and talking
- ■ Prefer diagrams/mind maps
- ■ No preference

[4]

Pages 15–18 **Research**

1. A random sample can be selected by putting the names of the target population into a hat or assigning each participant a number and putting the numbers into a computer random number generator. Set the parameters for how many participants you want and you then get your random sample. [2]

2. It is the least biased sampling method as every member of the target population has an equal chance of being chosen. It is also free from researcher bias. [2]

3. a) Stratified sampling should be more representative of the target population compared to a systematic sample because using systematic means taking every nth person from the register. This could result in every participant having one set of characteristics, such as being all men, so would not be representative. However, stratified sampling chooses a strata of the target population. For example, if your target population of people working in the college was 50% men and 50% women then your participants need to reflect this, making it more representative. [4]

b) They could put all the participants' names into a hat and pick out the first ten for example and they could be condition one, then the second ten could be in condition two. **[2]**

c) The colleague could have mentioned participant variables being an issue with an independent groups design. Using either a matched pairs design, matching people on relevant characteristics, or switching to a repeated measures design would eliminate this issue. **[4]**

d) An ethical issue could be informed consent. This is an issue as participants may need to drink alcohol if they are in the alcohol condition. They will need to be informed of this so they can agree. It could be a problem if they are intolerant to alcohol or are on medication that could have consequences if mixed with drink. Or they may simply not drink so they need informed consent so they have the right to withdraw before starting the study. **[4]**

e) The IV is the (one bottle of 300ml beer) alcohol or no alcohol conditions. **[2]**

f) The dependent variable, effect on driving, could be operationalised by using a driving simulation like in a theory driving test, to see the number of errors made. **[2]**

4. A potential extraneous variable could be the clarity of the driving video used. If it is unclear or too small, participants may not be able to see the hazards clearly and this affects their driving, not whether they have had alcohol. Or it could be the environment in which they sit the video, if it's too bright and they cannot see the screen properly this could also affect their driving skills on the hazard test. **[3]**

5. There will be a difference in the number of errors made in a driving simulation hazard test between participants who drank alcohol (a bottle of 300ml beer), compared to those who had no alcohol OR participants who drank alcohol will record more errors on a hazard test compared to those who drank no alcohol. **[3]**

6. a) The range is higher in the alcohol condition compared to the non-alcohol telling us that results were more consistent in the non-alcohol condition and more spread in the alcohol group. **[2]**

b) A problem with the range is that it is affected by anomalies. If there are extreme scores this extends the highest or lowest number and doesn't really tell us much information about the actual number of errors the participants made, only the difference between the highest and lowest score. **[2]**

7. a) A consent form includes all details about the study including the aims, the procedures, ethical issues that

will be addressed and a place for the participant to sign to agree to take part. **[2]**

b) Opportunity **[1]**

8. a) A lab experiment **[1]**

b) A strength of a lab experiment is it is a highly controlled environment. This means any extraneous variables have been controlled and won't affect results. This allows researchers to establish cause and effect. A weakness is that because of the controlled environment the study may have low validity as it isn't showing people's behaviour in real life, only under strict lab conditions. **[4]**

9. a) Field experiment **[1]**

b) A strength of a field experiment is that it occurs in a real environment therefore increasing the validity as it shows people's behaviour in everyday life. However there is no control over extraneous variables and therefore these can affect the results of the study. **[4]**

c) The difference between the two studies were that the lab experiment took place under highly controlled conditions, meaning no extraneous variables could affect the results, whereas scenario two was a field experiment meaning extraneous variables could not be controlled and could have affected results. However the scenario two environment is true to real life as it takes place in the real world, whereas scenario one does not. This means scenario two has high validity whereas scenario one has low validity. **[4]**

10. C

11. B

12. A

13. Primary data is collected first-hand by a researcher for the purpose of the study. Secondary data is where a researcher uses data that somebody else had collected i.e. reading about what research has found in a textbook. **[2]**

14. a) Data reordered: 41, 52, 53, 59, 64, 67, 72, 75, 75, 82, 88, 90, 95 **[1]**
Median = 72 **[1]**

b) 95 – 41 **[1]**
Range = 54 **[1]**

c) 75 **[1]**

15. a) 25 + 28 + 24 + 26 + 23 + 27 + 26 = 179 **[1]**
179 ÷ 7 = 25.57 (2 d.p.) **[1]**

b) (23 ÷ 35) × 100 = 65.714... **[1]**
= 66% (2 s.f.) **[1]**

c)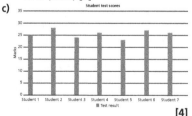
[4]

1. C

2. The number of people giving the wrong answer affects an individual's tendency to conform to the majority opinion. Asch's experiment involved a group of participants who were shown simple line comparison tasks. The participants were asked to indicate which of three comparison lines (labelled A, B, and C) matched a target line in length. The correct answer was always obvious. The participants were the last ones to give their answers after hearing the confederates' responses. Asch varied the number of confederates in each group. The presence of two confederates increased conformity to the wrong answer in 13.6% of the trails. Three confederates increased conformity to 31.8%. Once the group reached a certain size, around four, conformity did not continue to increase. **[3]**

3. Locus of control is a dispositional explanation of conformity as it refers to an individual's belief about the degree of control they have over their own life and the outcomes they experience. People with an internal locus of control believe that they have control over their own actions and the events that occur in their lives and are less likely to conform to the majority. They are more likely to resist conformity and maintain their independent judgements and behaviours. They do not need validation or approval from others. Whereas individuals with an external locus of control believe that external factors or forces, such as luck, fate, or powerful others, determine their outcomes. Having an external locus of control suggests a person is more likely to conform to the majority as they look to others to see how to act. As a result, they may be more likely to conform to group norms and conforming behaviours to fit in or avoid social disapproval. However, personality is only one factor that could play a part in conformity. There are other factors such as the situation a person is in. If the situation is a familiar one or the people are familiar, conformity could change depending on these social factors. When a situation is new or ambiguous, conformity may occur as the person is unsure how to act and therefore it is not due to their dispositional factors. **[6]**

4. Asch's line study aimed to investigate whether people would conform to the answers of a majority group, even when they are clearly incorrect. The procedure involved 123 participants, all men, tested with a group of 6-8 confederates. In any trial, there was only ever one real participant. The participants were shown a series of lines and asked to match a standard

line with one of the comparison lines. However, the majority of the confederates intentionally gave incorrect answers. 75% of the participants conformed to the incorrect majority opinion on at least one occasion during the study. 25% never conformed at all. Participants would often give incorrect answers to match the majority's responses, even when they were obviously wrong. The study showed the importance of social pressure on behaviour and the tendency for people to conform to judgements of a majority group, even when they knew those judgements were wrong. Asch's research demonstrated that people have a desire to fit in and avoid social disapproval. However, the Asch line study has limitations and has faced criticisms. Some argue that the study lacks validity as the task of comparing line lengths in a controlled laboratory setting may not fully represent real-world conformity situations. The pressure to conform in everyday life can be more complex. Additionally, cultural factors play a role in conformity levels, and the original study primarily focused on Western, individualistic cultures. Cultural differences may affect the extent to which individuals conform to group norms. It could be that the findings were a sign of the times in America in the 1950s, a period known as McCarthyism when people who acted outside of expected norms could be accused of being a spy with communist tendencies. Therefore people tried to fit in and not stand out. **[9]**

5. C
6. One strength of Milgram's agency theory is its ability to explain the high levels of obedience observed in Milgram's famous experiments. The theory offers insights into how individuals may willingly carry out harmful actions under the influence of perceived authority. It highlights the role of situational factors, such as the presence of an authority figure, in shaping behaviour. The theory provides an understanding of real-world instances of obedience to authority, such as in military settings and oppressive regimes. It helps explain why individuals may engage in morally questionable acts when they perceive themselves as acting on behalf of an authority figure. However, there are several limitations. Some argue that the theory may oversimplify the complexity of obedience. Human behaviour is influenced by a multitude of factors including personal values, moral principles, and social norms. Not all participants obeyed in Milgram's study, which shows there must be other explanations of obedience. It does not

explain why some individuals choose to defy authority or engage in acts of disobedience, even in situations where they may be in an agentic state. **[5]**

7. According to Adorno, individuals with an authoritarian personality exhibit several traits. These traits include sticking to social norms and values, a tendency to be submissive to authority figures, a rigid and inflexible mindset, a belief in the inherent superiority of certain social groups, and a high level of aggression towards those who deviate from established norms. Adorno believed that the authoritarian personality develops as a result of certain childhood experiences, that a combination of harsh and strict parenting, a strict adherence to traditional values, and a lack of critical thinking and independent exploration can contribute to the development of an authoritarian mindset. Individuals with an authoritarian personality have a specific cognitive style characterised by a black-and-white, dichotomous thinking pattern. They tend to view the world in terms of absolutes, categorising people and situations into rigid and simplistic categories of good or bad, right or wrong. **[3]**

8. C
9. A weakness of using questionnaires to assess personality type could be people giving socially desirable responses. If people don't give honest answers then the results will lack validity. **[2]**
10. In an interview, if you don't understand a question, you can ask the interviewer to clarify. With a questionnaire, if a person has been left to fill it out by themselves, they cannot check any questions they are unsure of. **[2]**
11. B
12. C
13. The presence of other people when a situation occurs results in less help being offered. People assume that others will help so stand back and don't help themselves. Also, some people are wary of helping as it may put them at risk of harm if the situation is a dangerous one. If the cost of helping outweighs the benefits, people are less likely to help. **[4]**
14. If the characteristics of the victim are similar to the bystander then they may be more likely to help. For example, in Piliavin's study, if the race of the victim was similar to the bystander then help was more likely. Expertise is another dispositional factor that can influence bystander intervention whereby if the bystander has medical knowledge that could help they would be more likely to intervene. **[4]**
15. A psychological state in which an individual experiences a loss of personal identity and a decrease in self-awareness when they are part of

a group or in a situation where their individuality is diminished. People may feel a reduced sense of personal responsibility and a decreased concern for the consequences of their actions, leading to a potential increase in impulsive and uninhibited behaviours. Contexts, such as during large gatherings, riots, football matches, or in situations where individuals are wearing uniforms or masks that conceal their identity, are more likely to see behaviour consistent with deindividuation. **[3]**

16. Personality is one dispositional factor affecting collective behaviour. For example, people with internal locus of control are less likely to lose their self-identity as they do not feel the need to look to others and are more likely to follow their own personal norms of behaviour. Morality is another dispositional factor affecting collective behaviour as some people have their own strong sense of moral values which means they will be less likely to follow the crowd. Their moral values will override any social norms being created by a crowd if they go against the person's own values and moral judgement. **[4]**

Pages 21–23 **Language, Thought and Communication**

1. C
2. A
3. Piaget's theory emphasises cognitive development in shaping language, whereas the Sapir-Whorf hypothesis suggests that language influences thought and perception. Piaget's theory of language focuses on the development of thinking and reasoning abilities in children and states that cognitive development precedes and shapes language development. Piaget's theory focuses on universal stages of cognitive development, while the Sapir-Whorf hypothesis explores the potential variations in cognition and perception across different languages and believes that the structure, vocabulary and concepts embedded within a language shape the way individuals think and perceive their experiences. **[4]**
4. Different languages may have distinct colour terminology, including the number and categorisation of colours. For example, some languages have separate words for different shades of a colour, while others may use more general terms. This can affect how individuals perceive and categorise colours, potentially leading to differences in colour recognition and memory. Cultural factors play a significant role in colour perception. Language is often influenced by cultural norms and

practices related to colour symbolism and meaning. These cultural influences can shape an individual's perception and memory of colours. For example, the Himba tribe have the same word for green and blue (bura) but use different words to distinguish between shades of green. When shown 11 green squares and one blue square, they had difficulty indicating which square was the odd one out but when shown 12 green squares, one of which was a lighter green, they had no problem identifying the odd one out. The Zuni people have one word for yellow and orange and in testing, when compared to English-speaking people, they had more problems in recall of those colours. **[4]**

5. The groups in the table have limited groups of colour, in particular the Dani people. If carrying out a recall task involving colour, the Dani people would struggle to perform well because of their limited naming of colours compared to English speakers. The same would be true of the Zuni and Berinmo. Therefore showing them a colour chart and asking them to recall the colours would be problematic. **[3]**

6. Using a questionnaire could pose problems for the different groups as if the variation language is more limited, compared to the English language, this could impact on the understanding of a questionnaire. If the questionnaire had been developed by English-speaking people the words used may not have the same meaning for the different groups. For example, a group of people living in one of the South Pacific islands use one word to mean a range of emotions of love, compassion and sadness. English speakers would find it difficult to understand the variation of emotions using just one word. **[3]**

7. Von Frisch, an ethologist, studied the dances performed by bees and suggested this was their way of communication. He wanted to understand the meaning of this dance and to understand how bees communicate information about food sources to their hive. He suggested that when the honeybees returned to their hives after finding a food source, they performed a series of movements known as the 'waggle' dance. The 'waggle' dance involves a figure-eight pattern, with the bee waggling its abdomen and vibrating its wings. The direction and duration of the dance convey information about the distance and direction of the food source relative to the position of the sun. Von Frisch demonstrated that honeybees rely on visual cues, such as the angle of the dance relative to gravity and the position of the sun, to interpret the information conveyed in the 'waggle' dance. **[4]**

8. Von Frisch's research on bee communication contributed to our understanding of animal communication. The research took place over many years, adding scientific credibility to the findings. The work earned him the Nobel Prize, the highest commendation in academia. However, Von Frisch did not study the sound that the bees made and it was discovered later that if the dance was performed without noise then other bees would not go to the food sources. Therefore this may be another form of communication that Von Frisch overlooked. He also found that not all bees did go to the food regardless of the dance or sound and so there must be other signals that the bees give that have yet to be discovered. But his work did have an impact on human understanding of animal communication. **[4]**

9.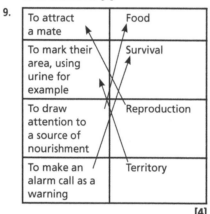

[4]

10. One thing that human communication has that animals do not is the ability to plan ahead. For example, we can make plans with each other and put important events in a diary but animals cannot do this. **[2]**

11. Gestures, for example, beating its chest. **[1]**

12. Inter-observer reliability could be a problem in the observation if only one researcher is observing. The observer could be biased in what they record and this could make findings unreliable. In order to improve the reliability, the observer would need another observer to carry out the same observation. They could each have a table of behavioural categories to look out for. This would have been devised by them already so they both know what they are looking for. Each time they see a behaviour in the table they would put a tally mark. At the end of the observation they can compare the tallies to see if they agree. **[4]**

13. A strength of an observation is that real behaviour is being observed by another person, in an objective way. It is not reliant on self-reporting which could give a biased view by the participant themselves. Therefore

observation has higher validity. A weakness of observations is that they can be affected by observer bias. The observer may record behaviour that they want to see that fits their hypothesis. In this way, the expectations of the researcher have an effect on the findings. **[4]**

14. Verbal communication is anything that is written or spoken in words. For example, having a conversation with someone or writing a text message is verbal communication. Non-verbal communication is communication without the use of words. For example, facial expressions to show happiness (smiling) or anger (scowling). **[4]**

15. Three functions of eye contact are: to regulate the flow of conversation, this shows the person who you are speaking with that you are interested in what they are saying. To signal attraction, for example, we may look at someone and catch their eye if we like a person. To express emotion, for example, when people are upset the eye contact can be quite intense. **[3]**

16. a) Opportunity **[1]**

b) The participants appeared to use eye contact to regulate the conversation flow as when one person stopped speaking they would look at the other person. This would signal they had finished speaking and then they would expect the other person to speak. As in the study above, when the person was ready to speak they would break eye contact, giving signals they were about to talk. **[4]**

c) The people could be randomly paired by putting all the names into a hat and pulling out the first name followed by the second name and they are the first pair. Then continue to do this until all the participants are paired. **[2]**

d) A covert observation is hidden. This means the participants are unaware they are being observed. The researcher will be watching from a hidden place. **[2]**

e) One ethical issue with covert observations is the lack of informed consent. As people are unaware they are being watched they cannot give their consent. This is a problem because if they were made aware they may not agree to be observed. People should have the right to refuse to participate. **[2]**

f) It could be concluded that eye contact regulates the flow of conversation as the people in the cafe would use their eyes to give a prolonged look to show when they had finished speaking. They also used them to show when they were about to speak, by breaking eye contact. **[3]**

17. Postural echo, also known as mirroring or mimicry, refers to the subconscious imitation of another person's body posture, gestures or movements. It is a non-verbal behaviour where an individual unintentionally mimics the postures and movements of another person they are interacting with. **[2]**

18. Closed posture is when a person pulls themselves close to their own body when interacting with someone else. For example, crossing their arms or legs. It is thought to happen when a person doesn't feel very comfortable or as a way of rejecting the other person. Open posture is relaxed and shows the person is completely at ease. **[2]**

19. Cultural norms can affect personal space and touch. For example, in some cultures it is completely acceptable to stand up close and personal to another person, even if they are not very familiar with each other. In other cultures this would come across as an invasion of personal space and unacceptable as it may make the person feel uncomfortable. It has been found that English people prefer a personal space of about 1.5m whereas Arabs are comfortable a lot closer together. **[2]**

20.

Factor affecting personal space	Description
Culture	Differences for personal space between cultures. For example, English prefer 1.5m distance but Arabs are comfortable with less distance.
Status	People who are of similar status are comfortable standing close together, compared to those who are unequal in status.
Gender	Men appear to prefer a bigger social distance compared to women. With friends, men still prefer to sit opposite their friend whereas women will sit closer, side-by-side.

[6]

21. Darwin believed that non-verbal communication was an innate, evolutionary mechanism; it has evolved and is adaptive. All mammals show emotions through facial expression and the behaviour is universal and therefore evolutionary.

Non-verbal behaviours persist in humans because they have been acquired for their value throughout evolutionary history. For example, showing anger, which could signal to others to stay away from potential harm. **[4]**

22. Non-verbal behaviour appears to be innate. For example, children who have been blind since birth show the same facial expressions as sighted children. A study of sighted and blind judo athletes found that both groups produced the same facial expressions in certain emotional situations, suggesting the behaviour is innate as the blind students would have been unable to learn the expressions. This supports the evolutionary theory of non-verbal behaviour. **[4]**

23. Yuki investigated cultural differences in the perception and interpretation of facial expressions, specifically focusing on the role of the eyes and mouth as cues for recognising emotions. The study compared participants from Japan and the United States. Over several trials, participants were shown photographs of facial expressions with varying combinations of eye and mouth expressions. They were then asked to identify the emotion being displayed. The results indicated that Japanese participants paid more attention to the eyes when interpreting emotions, whilst American participants focused more on the mouth region. The study examined the impact of culture on the recognition of emotions conveyed through emoticons. The study was criticised for not using real faces, so could lack in validity and applying findings to real life interpretations of facial expressions could be difficult. The findings revealed that Japanese participants were better at identifying emotions expressed through emoticons compared to American participants. This highlighted cultural differences in the interpretation of facial expressions and the role of different facial cues in emotion recognition. It also shed light on the cross-cultural understanding of emoticons and their usage as a form of non-verbal communication. **[6]**

Pages 24–26 **Brain and Neuropsychology**

1. D
2. A
3. B
4. B
5. C
6. The somatic nervous system is responsible for voluntary control of skeletal muscles. It allows individuals to consciously initiate and control movements, such as walking, talking, or writing. In contrast, the autonomic nervous system regulates involuntary functions, such as heartbeat, digestion, respiration, and glandular activity. These processes occur automatically and are not under conscious control. The autonomic nervous system is further divided into two branches, the sympathetic nervous system and the parasympathetic nervous system. The sympathetic branch prepares the body for "fight-or-flight" responses during times of stress or danger, while the parasympathetic branch promotes relaxation, rest and digestion. The somatic nervous system has no subdivisions. **[2]**

7. The fight-or-flight response is a physiological and psychological reaction triggered in response to a perceived threat or stressful situation. The response begins with the brain's recognition of a potential threat or danger. The hypothalamus detects the stressor and activates the sympathetic branch of the autonomic nervous system. This triggers the release of a stress hormone adrenaline, from the adrenal glands, into the bloodstream. The release of adrenaline produces several physiological changes in the body, preparing it for action. These changes include, amongst others, increased heart rate to pump more oxygenated blood to the muscles and vital organs, rapid breathing to increase oxygen and dilation of the pupils. The fight-or-flight response enhances mental alertness, attention, and sensory perception. Non-essential bodily functions, such as digestion and immune response, are temporarily suppressed to allocate resources to more immediate survival needs. The response mobilises energy resources in the body to support physical exertion. At the same time as the signal for the sympathetic branch is triggered, the hypothalamic-adrenal (HPA) axis is activated. This pathway is much slower so the effects are delayed. This pathway leads to the release of cortisol, a stress hormone that helps to sustain the body's stress response. This HPA returns the body to its resting state once the stressor has passed. **[5]**

8. A hormone

9. The James-Lange theory of emotion suggests that emotions are a result of our bodily reactions to external stimuli. According to the theory, an external event or stimulus triggers a physiological response in the body. This could be a visual, auditory or sensory input that we perceive through our senses. The physiological response comes before the experience of emotion. The body reacts to the stimulus by producing specific physiological changes, such as increased heart rate, sweaty palms or a racing pulse. Our conscious experience of emotion is a result of perceiving and interpreting the

physiological changes in our body. For example, if you encounter a spider in the bath and you don't like spiders, the heart rate will increase and the palms of your hands may get sweaty. This is interpreted as fear, leading to the experience of fear itself. **[4]**

10. C
11. A
12. Synaptic transmission is where information is transmitted from one neuron to another across a synapse. The electrical signals, known as action potentials, are converted into chemical signals and then transmitted to the post-synaptic neuron. When an electrical signal, known as an action potential, reaches the pre-synaptic terminal of a neuron, it causes synaptic vesicles, small sacs containing neurotransmitters, to fuse with the pre-synaptic membrane. This fusion releases the neurotransmitters into the synapse, the small gap between the pre-synaptic and post-synaptic neurons. The released neurotransmitter molecules diffuse across the synaptic cleft and bind to specific receptors located on the post-synaptic membrane. The binding of neurotransmitters to the receptors results in the generation of a post-synaptic potential, which can be excitatory or inhibitory depending on the type of neurotransmitter and receptor involved. Excitatory post-synaptic potentials (EPSPs) increase the likelihood of generating an action potential, while inhibitory post-synaptic potentials (IPSPs) decrease the likelihood of generating an action potential. **[5]**

13. Hebb's theory suggests that if one neuron consistently activates another, the synapse between them becomes stronger, facilitating communication between the two neurons. When we learn, neurons make new neural connections with other neurons and the more that information is visited the stronger the connections become. Hebb's theory suggests that we have synaptic plasticity, which refers to the ability of synapses to change their strength based on neural activity. When a pre-synaptic neuron repeatedly and consistently stimulates a post-synaptic neuron, the synapse between them undergoes long-term potentiation, leading to a strengthening of the connection between the two neurons which promotes learning and memory formation. **[7]**

14. The frontal lobe deals with thinking and planning. The motor cortex is in the frontal lobe of the brain, as is Broca's area. The motor cortex deals with voluntary movement. Broca's area, usually only in the left hemisphere, plays a role in the production of speech. The parietal lobe contains the somatosensory cortex which deals with incoming sensory information. The occipital lobe is at the back of the brain and contains the visual area dealing with visual information from the eyes. The temporal lobe contains the auditory cortex, which deals with sound-based information. The temporal lobe contains Wernicke's area which processes language comprehension. **[6]**

15.

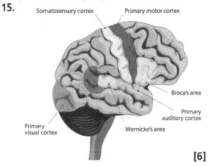

Somatosensory cortex
Primary motor cortex
Broca's area
Primary auditory cortex
Primary visual cortex
Wernicke's area

[6]

16. Cognitive neuroscience is the joining together of biological structures with mental processes and involves studying the influence of the brain's structure on cognitions and behaviour. Cognitive neuroscience uses brain scanning to map which areas of the brain are active when doing a particular activity, e.g. mapping activity in the motor cortex when voluntary movement is happening. This supports the idea that the brain is localised – that particular areas have a particular function. **[3]**

17.

	fMRI	PET	CT
How it works	Measures changes in blood flow	Measures metabolic activity	Produces X-ray images
What it does	Captures brain activity in real time	Measures brain function and activity	Provides detailed structural images
Resolution	High	Low	High
Exposure to radiation	No	Uses radioactive tracers	Uses X-ray radiation

18. Tulving's study wanted to find out whether episodic memories caused blood flow to different areas of the brain compared to when thinking about semantic memories. Volunteers were injected with radioactive gold which would get picked up on a PET scan. The participants took part in eight trials carrying out four each of both episodic (thinking about childhood holidays for example) and semantic tasks (recalling historical facts). Tulving found that blood flow was in different places depending on the task they were completing. Semantic information was taking place in the posterior cortex and the frontal lobe was more active when they were using episodic memories. **[4]**

19. Neurological damage such as a stroke can cause the area in which it occurred to die. This can result in disruption of function, which can be temporary or permanent. After trauma to the brain, some people can regain functions when another area picks up that particular function. For example, if the stroke or damage occurs in the motor area then walking could be a problem. If the damage occurs in the left hemisphere of the brain then Broca's area could be affected and speech may be affected (Broca's aphasia). If the damage is in the left temporal lobe then Wernicke's area could be affected and the person may struggle to understand language. **[4]**

Pages 27–30
Psychological Problems

1. It is predicted that by 2030 there will be two million more people in the world with mental health problems, compared to 2013. Women are more likely to be treated for mental health issues than men and this is becoming more of a significant gap. **[2]**

2. One reason could be the way lifestyles have changed over the years. There is a bigger gap in socio-economic status with the poorest people getting poorer which will affect mental health. Social isolation is also becoming more of a feature of modern living and that can play a part in mental health problems. **[2]**

3. Culture affects the way people think about poor mental health. For example, in some cultures hearing voices is seen as a way of communicating with spirits of the deceased whereas in the Western world it would be considered to be a disorder such a schizophrenia. **[2]**

4. One characteristic of good mental health is a positive self-attitude. This is where a person would be deemed to have good mental health if they have high self-esteem and view themselves in a positive light. Another characteristic is having an accurate perception of reality. People who find it difficult to face up to reality can suffer from disorders such as schizophrenia where they lose touch with reality. **[2]**

5. The language used to describe mental health issues has changed over the years which has helped to reduce the stigma. High-profile people have spoken openly about their mental health problems to help normalise various illnesses. **[2]**

6. a) Any factor such as work, school, loneliness, technology **[1]**
   b) We could assume that that there is a positive relationship between depression and life events but one does not cause the other. Only that when one is experienced the other is frequently present at the same time. **[2]**
   c) In this study, the researcher could collect qualitative data by asking the participants to keep a diary. This way they could record how

they are feeling on a daily basis and note down whether there were particular things that triggered their feelings. They could also say how they were feeling rather than just giving a score. **[3]**

d)

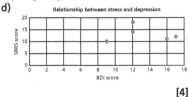

[4]

7. Unipolar depression is when a person presents with the one emotional state of feeling depressed with low mood continuously. Bipolar depression is when the person can fluctuate between feelings of low mood and depression and heightened states of mania, feeling and behaving in a frenzied way. **[2]**

8. The classifications are updated frequently to keep up-to-date with new behaviours or symptoms to ensure that people are getting appropriate treatments. **[2]**

9. One strength of using the ICD to diagnose unipolar depression is to ensure a valid diagnosis is made. The classification system allows for a checklist of behaviours to be compared against the person's symptoms to ensure the correct diagnosis is made. This ensures that a diagnosis is as objective as it can be and should mean that, if a different doctor was to carry out an assessment, they would reach the same diagnosis. **[3]**

10. C

11. D

12. A

13. One strength of the biological explanation of depression is its emphasis on the role of neurotransmitters and brain chemistry. Research has shown that imbalances in neurotransmitters such as serotonin are associated with depression. This has led to the development of effective drug treatments, such as selective serotonin reuptake inhibitors (SSRIs) that target these imbalances and help alleviate symptoms in many individuals. However, the biological explanation simplifies the complex nature of depression by focusing on biological factors and neglecting the influence of other explanations, such as cognitive ones. Depression is a multifaceted illness that can be influenced by other factors; attributing depression to biological causes overlooks other vitally important reasons for the depression. **[4]**

14. C

15. One strength of the psychological explanation of depression is its focus on individual experiences, thoughts and emotions. It recognises the significance of psychological processes, such as negative cognitive patterns, in the development and maintenance of depression. By addressing these psychological factors, therapeutic approaches like cognitive-behavioural therapy (CBT) can be effective in helping individuals manage and overcome depressive symptoms. A weakness of the psychological explanation is that it may overlook the role of biological factors in depression. Psychological factors may be important, but there is also evidence suggesting that biological factors, such as neurotransmitter imbalances and genetic predispositions, contribute to the development of depression. This may limit the effectiveness of psychological interventions for individuals whose depression has a strong biological component. **[4]**

16. Biological interventions such as antidepressant medications, SSRIs, are commonly prescribed to help regulate neurotransmitter levels in the brain and alleviate depressive symptoms. Serotonin is released by one neuron and binds to receptors on the post-synaptic neuron, transmitting signals. After the transmission, serotonin is taken back up by the releasing neuron through a process called reuptake. SSRIs work by blocking the reuptake process. By doing so, it allows serotonin to remain in the synaptic gap between neurons for a longer time, giving it more to bind. SSRIs can be effective in reducing symptoms of depression but may have side effects and require careful monitoring. They quickly block the reuptake but the symptoms do not start to lessen for at least three months which is puzzling if this is the only reason for the depression. There is no commitment for drug treatment so it is relatively easy to engage with. This treatment could be considered to take a reductionist approach as it is only targeting the neurotransmitter serotonin and not looking at anything else as the cause. This may explain why the treatment doesn't work for everyone, if the cause is something other than serotonin. CBT is a psychological therapy for depression that targets the way someone with depression thinks. The belief is that if the negative thinking is changed, the behaviour will change. The treatment gets the patient involved by encouraging them to take part in an activity that they used to enjoy for example. They try and deal with the negative patterns of thinking during the therapy sessions by disputing the negative and sometimes irrational thoughts. Patients are also asked to keep a diary so any triggers can be identified. One strength of CBT is that the patient has control over their treatment unlike drugs where it is not within the patient's hands as to how they respond. The treatment also takes a holistic approach, examining different factors that might be the underlying cause of the depression such as work or family life. The person is encouraged to assess any changes they could implement which could improve their life and subsequently their depression. Once a person has been through CBT they can use the strategies again by themselves in future if needed. **[9]**

17. Addiction refers to a behaviour that leads to dependency. For example, an addiction to alcohol results in a dependency where individuals feel that they are unable to survive without it. However, substance misuse results in the substance being taken to excess but does not necessarily lead to addiction, they don't feel unable to survive if they don't have it. **[2]**

18. It could be argued that Cary is showing signs of substance misuse as she is not following the rules for her medication because she is taking double the prescribed dosage. It could be that she is also showing a dependence as she is relying on the tablets to manage her pain. She could build up a tolerance to the pills that could result in side effects and eventually addiction. **[4]**

19. D

20. A genetic vulnerability is where a person inherits a particular gene that increases the risk of a certain behaviour or characteristic. However having a vulnerability does not determine that an addiction will occur, only that it predisposes the person to that behaviour. **[2]**

21. To investigate genetic explanations of addiction researchers will use twin or family studies. Identical twins are 100% the same and therefore it is easier to identify a particular gene playing a part in addictions. By comparing twins, both monozygotic (MZ) identical and dizygotic (DZ) non-identical, natural experiments can be used to see if addictions are genetically inherited. **[3]**

22. Looking at twin studies is problematic as the twins have usually been brought up together in the same environment. This means it is difficult to separate the influence of nature or nurture. Also families can often treat twins exactly the same which makes it less clear regarding the influence of nature or nurture. **[2]**

23. Kaij studied male twins from Sweden and conducted interviews to find out about their alcohol use. Kaij found that from 48 MZ twins and 126 DZ twins, who were registered with a society to reduce their consumption of alcohol, 61% of the MZ twins were concordant in being registered with the group, compared to 39% of the DZ twins. **[4]**

24. Kaij's study supports the theory that alcohol consumption is linked

to genetics because there were significantly more MZ twins seeking support than DZ. **[2]**

25. Ashley is showing a dependence on alcohol because she is beginning to prioritise alcohol over other things such as being with her old friends. She is also showing signs that it is becoming the most important thing to her as she is spending too much money and having to borrow more so she can go out drinking. **[3]**

26. A psychological explanation would suggest that through social learning theory, Ashley is vicariously learning that drinking with her friends is fun. She sees the fun they have and is learning vicariously that she can enjoy the same feelings of pleasure when out socialising and drinking. This gives her the rewards of being sociable and potentially popular with her work colleagues. She has imitated their drinking culture and, as they are of a similar age to Ashley, she is imitating their behaviour. The social norms in her new work place are such that socialising out of work and drinking is the behaviour that people engage in. Ashley may also have gained a new social identity in that she now feels she belongs to this new group of friends, whereas she no longer feels so close to her old friends. **[4]**

Practice Exam Papers

Pages 31–44 **Practice Exam Paper 1 Cognition and Behaviour**

A Memory

01 B
02 When we store information, we don't remember everything **[1]** so when we go to recall it, we fill in any gaps so it makes sense (using schemas, beliefs etc.) **[1]**
03 A lack of standardisation of procedures can lead to a lack of validity in research **[1]**. In Bartlett's research, participants having no clear idea of what they had to do in the series of studies could have affected the results therefore reducing the validity of his findings on reconstructive memory. **[1]**
04.1 Interference is affecting Stella
04.2 If Stella plays basketball first, the rules of this could interfere with her playing netball afterwards as they are similar sports but the rules are different such as running with the ball). **[1]** She may then run with the ball in netball (which isn't allowed) and could get penalised **[1]**; this could cause her friends to get frustrated with her **[1]** and they could lose matches because of the interference of the two similar sports. **[1]**
05.1 Students are convinced they will do well because of context acting as a prompt **[1]**. They feel that doing exams in their learning classroom

will act as a cue and this will increase the accuracy of their memory. **[1]** The classroom may help to prompt a memory of something they learned in the room and this will enhance their memory. **[1]** Other factors, such as emotional states, can also act as a cue to affect recall. **[1]**
Research to support context was carried out showing that divers learning word lists and recalling them either in the same or different environment affected accuracy. **[1]** When the recall environment mirrored the learning environment, e.g. learning words on the beach and recalling them on the beach, recall was superior compared to when they learned the words on the beach but recalled them under water. **[1]** This evidence supports context as a cue for memory. However, the recall was carried out immediately and in real life we don't usually have to recall immediately after learning things. **[1]** In school there is significant time lapse between learning and recall in exams, so this supporting evidence has its weaknesses. **[1]** However, we do know that when we struggle to recall information, cues such as the first letter of someone's name do prompt recall so the theory does have validity in real life. **[1]**
05.2 Episodic memories are memories of events in a person's life **[1]** e.g. the first day at secondary school. These are time-stamped so more details are recalled such as the time of year or who else was there. **[1]** Semantic memories are memories of all the facts and knowledge a person has learned over their life e.g. knowing London is the capital city of England. **[1]** These memories are not time-stamped so you won't remember when you learned the information. **[1]** Procedural memories are skills that we learn, how to do something e.g. riding a bike. **[1]** These memories are implicit as we know how to do the skill but cannot explain afterwards how we do it. **[1]**

B Perception

06 C
07 **One** mark for **any one** of the following:
Height in plane
Relative size
Occlusion
Linear perspective
08.1 Size constancy is the ability to perceive objects as being the same size, even if we are viewing them at a distance. **[1]** It helps maintain a stable and accurate perception of the world because objects at a distance will produce a retinal image that will be smaller, but the brain will perceive the object's size as constant **[1]** e.g. when looking out of a window of a

tall building, the cars below will look small but our brain will retain the size of them. **[1]**
08.2 **One** mark for either:
Retinal disparity **[1]** or Convergence **[1]**
Retinal disparity occurs because the view we see from each eye is different due to the distance between our eyes (about 6cm); **[1]** the closer the object is, the bigger the retinal disparity; **[1]** the further away the object is, the smaller the retinal disparity. **[1]**
Convergence is when we view an object close up and our eyes converge (turn inwards); **[1]** the muscles work harder when the object is closer and it's this information that gives the brain the information regarding distance and depth. **[1]** The further away the object is, our muscles can relax and we look straight ahead. **[1]**
09 Bruner and Minturn's findings have real-life application as they help to explain why we sometimes make mistakes even when the stimulus is right in front of us; **[1]** e.g. if you're reading something about rabbits and there's an error and the word rabbi is written instead, you may continue to read it as rabbit as this is what you expect to be written. **[1]** However, the study does not account for individual differences as it used an independent group design that may affect the study's validity as people in one group may have had key differences to people in the other group. **[1]** In real life we wouldn't usually look at ambiguous figures and therefore these findings may not be applied to a real-life setting so are low in validity. **[1]**
10 Gregory believed that we construct the world around us by making an interpretation of what we are seeing, based on information from our past experiences. **[1]** This suggests that perception develops more from nurture than nature. **[1]** Sometimes when we lack some details or information, our brain fills in the gaps (using inferences). **[1]** This allows us to construct an idea of what we are seeing based on previous sensory experiences. **[1]**
11.1 Gibson's theory suggests that perception is innate and has evolved and that no learning is required. **[1]** We don't need to perceive anything as everything we sense is detailed enough and allows us to judge distance and depth without any interpretation being needed. **[1]** When we move, our brain receives this information, via optic flow patterns, so movement and direction can be judged. **[1]** e.g. when we are travelling in a car, the visual image we receive changes, objects that are closer appear to move faster as we

go past them while things that are further away appear to move slowly (motion parallax). [1]

11.2 Gibson's theory can support the nature side of the nature-nurture debate through an experiment that was carried out on young babies. [1] The visual cliff was devised and tested six-month-old babies on the edge of what looked like a drop off a cliff, but the drop was covered in a see-through Perspex screen. [1] Even though the infants were encouraged to crawl across by their mothers, most wouldn't, showing this behaviour to be innate, not learned. [1] Gibson suggested this supported his theory as no learning was necessary for the babies to perceive depth. [1]

C Development

12.1 C
12.2 D
13.1 B
13.2 A
13.3 **One** mark for **any one** of the following:
Egocentrism is a feature of children's cognition; [1] they are unable to put themselves in the position of another mentally, physically or emotionally; [1] they are selfish. [1]
Plus one mark for: Children only see things from their own perspective, they are unable to take on anyone else's view. [1]
14.1 Kane is in the pre-operational stage
14.2 Tulula is showing a reduction in egocentrism as she is able to take on another perspective. [1] She understands hide and seek involves the other person not being able to see her at all. [1] Unlike Kane who can be seen, Tulula hides fully. [1]
15.1 Covert observation [1]
The children will behave naturally and not differently as they would if they were in front of an observer. [1] Choose **any two** behaviours e.g. child cannot share a ball; [1] cannot take turns in a game [1]
Informed consent [1]
As they are children under the age of 16, informed consent must be gained from the parent or guardian prior to the study being carried out. [1]
15.2 **Any two** points from the following:
A fixed mindset is someone who will give up. [1] They will see no point in trying to do well as failure is evidence they cannot do it. [1] No amount of effort will make any difference, [1] intelligence is fixed, [1] ability is passed down through a person's genes. [1]
15.3 Carlos is a kinaesthetic learner [1]. He prefers to physically do work, such as making videos, rather than reading his notes. [1] Mina is a visual learner. [1] She prefers to use images and diagrams for her revision. [1] Jamal is a verbaliser. [1] He demonstrates this

as he prefers to write his notes more than once as he prefers words. [1]
15.4 C

D Research Methods

16.1 The ethical issue is protection from harm. [1] Serena could protect the participants from feeling embarrassed by ensuring their details are kept confidential. [1] She could use their initials or a number [1] as this would ensure no-one knew about their beliefs about UFOs. [1]
16.2 A weakness is that responses may lack detail because they use closed questions [1] which means no in-depth information will be gathered. [1]
17.1 Qualitative
17.2 A structured interview contains pre-set closed questions [1] that will be asked in order to follow a script that has been prepared [1] whereas an unstructured interview may have one or two prepared questions that are open [1] but the interview develops in response to the answers. [1]
17.3 There will be a correlation [1] between the confidence score /10 and the score /10 in the belief of UFOs. [1]
17.4 Positive correlation
17.5 A strength is that it allows a starting point for more research [1] because it could tell us that these two variables are related (that the more confident people are, the more likely they believe in UFOs). [1] This could lead to understanding how these variables are related (people who are confident might feel they are more able to admit to their beliefs). [1]
18.1 **One** mark for title e.g. scattergraph of a correlation between confidence levels and beliefs of UFO. [1] **One** mark for labelled axis e.g. belief in UFO s /10. [1] **One** mark for labelled axis e.g confidence score /10. [1] Appropriate plots not joined up. [1]

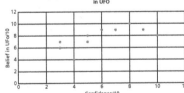

18.2 The mode for confidence is 3 + 5
18.3 The mode for belief is 9
18.4 C
18.5 A

> **Pages 45–57 Practice Exam Paper 2 Social Context and Behaviour**

A Social Influence

01 B
2.1 Lilah thinks Tom conforms due to group size. [1] This is because she says

he waits for at least three people to answer and this is the number Asch suggested is optimum for conformity to occur. [1]
2.2 Lilah claims to only conform when she finds questions too difficult which is more likely in an ambiguous situation. [1] This is because people often lack confidence in their own ability. [1] Asch found when the stimulus line was made more similar to the comparison line, conformity increased. [1]
3.1 100%
3.2 Milgram suggested a social explanation of obedience, such as the role of authority having an influence. [1] He suggested that if someone is perceived as having the right to tell you what to do, by wearing a uniform for example, then obedience is more likely. [1] Adorno on the other hand suggested a person's disposition or personality influenced obedience. [1] Adorno suggested this was due to their upbringing that made them more likely to obey someone who is superior to them. [1]
4.1 The IV in Piliavin's study was the victim being drunk; [1] drunk was described as smelling of alcohol and carrying a brown bag with a bottle of alcohol. [1] The second independent variable was being disabled; [1] this was defined as walking with a cane. [1]
4.2 Through observation
4.3 The observer could have been biased (to support a diffusion of responsibility hypothesis) e.g. by noting down that a passenger did not help when they may have tried to but could not get to where the victim was; [1] this could make findings low in validity. [1] Or If the carriage was crowded/view obstructed, the observers may not have seen properly what was happening [1] so relevant data could have been missed giving low validity of findings. [1] Or the observers had a lot of data to record and they may have missed something [1], so data was unreliable. [1]
5.1 Deindividuation. [1] This is when people lose their sense of self-identity through things e.g. wearing a uniform/being part of a big crowd. [1]
5.2 Deindividuation affects collective behaviour through individuals becoming anonymous. [1] When people go into a deindividuated state they lose their sense of self, behaving in ways they may not normally behave. [1] This often occurs when part of a crowd, such as being at a demonstration. [1] Zimbardo found in his studies that when participants were given a uniform such as hoods to hide their faces, they were more likely to deliver an electric shock to another person. [1] This was in comparison to participants who wore their own clothing and were less likely to do this. [1]

B Language, Thought and Communication

06 Language can influence the way in which people remember events. Nonsense pictures, paired with a label, were shown to two groups. The label was different for each group. [1] When asked to draw the picture from memory, it was found that the label had influenced the participants' memory of it. [1] Recognition of colour is influenced by language as seen by The Zuni who only use one term for the yellow-orange region of the colour spectrum. [1] When Zuni participants were shown a coloured chip and asked to locate it amongst other chips, they performed better if there was a simple colour name (e.g. red) rather than a mixture of red and blue showing language can affect recall in different cultures. [1]

07 Research into personal space is often carried out without the informed consent from the participant. [1] For example, this is an ethical issue because if they knew what they were participating in and how they would react when people get close to them, they may not want to take part [1] as it may not portray them in a positive light if they move away. Another ethical issue is the right to withdraw. [1] If the participant doesn't know they are taking part, they can't withdraw their data even if they felt uncomfortable if people were too close to them. [1]

08

Planning ahead	B
Leave pheromones	A
Use communication for specific events	A
Advertise fitness	A

09 D

10 Piaget said children need to be at the right stage of their cognitive development in order to understand words otherwise they will just say words they don't understand. [1] He suggested they develop language in the sensorimotor stage, at the end of their first year. Before this they develop schema, which is a mental representation about the world e.g. a child develops a schema for a cat that begins as something that is furry, purrs and has four legs before learning the name, cat. Children develop language by matching words to their existing knowledge/schema as they understand the concept first and then learn the words. [1] In the pre-operational stage, children learn language rapidly and they can talk in sentences. In the concrete operational stage, their language matures and becomes more logical. [1] It is difficult to prove Piaget's theory as we have no way of knowing if someone has a schema or not. [1] However, language appears not to be random e.g. a child might say "Teddy shoe" to show the shoe is owned by them. This shows schemas are being used to build language. [1] However, Sapir and Whorf said it was impossible to think about things if we have no words for it, we only think about things that we have the words for. [1] There is supporting evidence for the Sapir-Whorf hypothesis, such as the variation in recognition of colours and recall of events. [1] For example, the Berinmo have problems recognising different colours because they only have five words for them [1] limiting their ability to recognise a range of colours. This supports the Sapir and Whorf hypothesis as Berinmo cannot recognise the colours they have no words for. [1]

11 Yuki wanted to see if emoticons are understood differently by people in Japan compared to America. [1] 95 Japanese and 118 American students took part and were shown six sad, happy or neutral emoticons. [1] Using a 9-point happiness scale, Japanese participants gave higher ratings to faces with happy eyes, even when the mouth was sad. The opposite was found with the American participants (higher ratings when mouths were happy even when the eyes were sad). [1]

C Brain and Neuropsychology

12 A Spinal cord [1], B Autonomic nervous system [1], C Sympathetic or parasympathetic [1], D Parasympathetic or sympathetic [1]

13 C

14.1 fMRI [1], CT [1] and PET scans [1]

14.2 fMRI [1]

14.3 fMRI does not use radiation which is a strength of this scanning technique. [1] It also shows almost live activity as it occurs. [1] However, it is expensive to use [1] so there may be cheaper alternatives that might be more cost effective. [1]

15 Hebb's theory has scientific support from recent research and advances in cognitive neuroscience. [1] His theory has provided useful application to real life such as in education where some of the principles are utilised, such as practising information (rehearsal) to strengthen neural pathways which form memories. [1] However, Hebb's theory only looks at structural changes in the brain during learning, whilst ignoring cognitive processes. [1] This reductionism is seen as a weakness of his theory because it attempts to explain the complexity of learning by mainly focusing on brain activity. [1]

16 Left hemisphere

17 Parietal lobe

18 Cognitive neuroscience is the combination of biology (brain activity/biological structures) and mental processes (such as perception, learning and memory) used to explain the neurobiological basis of thought processes and disorders. [1] With the introduction and improvements in technology such as fMRI, CT and PET scans, science has been able to investigate live brains, unlike previously where it was reliant on post-mortems. [1] Research, such as Tulving's study using PET scans, has shown the neurological basis of mental processes where different types of memories are located in different areas of the brain. [1] This has helped us to understand how neurological damage in a particular area of the brain can affect different abilities. [1] So if a person has a brain injury to their frontal lobe, their episodic memories could be affected. [1] Strokes that occur in the left hemisphere could result in loss of speech (Broca's aphasia) or loss of language comprehension (Wernicke's aphasia). Cognitive neuroscience has helped science to understand neurological damage and its impact on behaviour. [1]

D Psychological Problems

19 A [1] and C [1]

20 One individual effect could be damage to relationships. [1] Partner, family and friend relationships can often be damaged or even break down because the individual wants to isolate themselves, unable to cope with social interaction. [1] Or An individual effect could be not being able to cope with everyday tasks and living. [1] Things that people take for granted, such as getting out of bed in the morning and taking a shower can become a problem for an individual with mental health problems. [1] Or Physical well-being can also be affected by mental health problems. [1] For example, when people are mentally unwell this usually makes them suffer with stress. When we suffer long-term stress, it impacts our immune system and leaves us more vulnerable to physical illnesses such as colds. [1]

21.1 Opportunity [1] as they happened to be there at the clinic, were available at the time and agreed to take part. [1]

21.2 8 [1] 5, 6, 7, 8, 8, 8, 9, 9, 10, 10 [1]

21.3 The results suggest that the treatment the patients were undergoing was effective [1] as all patients gave a lower score out of ten after six months. [1] However, the median score after six months is only two lower than the original median score [1] which could suggest we cannot draw conclusions about how effective the treatment was. [1]

21.4 The patients could have been given antidepressants. [1] These could have side-effects such as weight gain or sleeping problems, which can make them undesirable to take. **[1]** However, they are thought to be effective in over 50% of patients, although about 25-30% of people taking placebos also report improvements. **[1]** This makes it difficult to assess how effective they really are. **[1]** They are not suitable for everyone, e.g. children, and they only treat the symptoms not the cause. **[1] Or** The patients could have been given CBT. **[1]** This has no side-effects, which can make it seem a more desirable treatment. **[1]** However, it is not suitable for severe cases of depression and usually the best treatment is a combination of drugs and CBT. **[1]** CBT requires commitment from the patient, attending regular sessions, so may not be suitable for everyone **[1]** but it is seen as a more holistic therapy that aims to treat the symptoms and the cause of the depression. **[1]**

22 Based on social learning theory, DeBlasio and Benda (1993) found, in adolescents, the influence of peers play a big part in taking alcohol and drugs. **[1]** For example, observing other teenagers who smoke, influences them to smoke. **[1]** They are more likely to associate with other adolescents who smoke, with adolescent risk taking more likely to occur in a group situation. **[1]** This shows that social learning can explain the influence of others and imitation of behaviour to occur. **[1]**

Acknowledgements

The authors and publisher are grateful to the copyright
holders for permission to use quoted materials and images.

All images © Shutterstock.com

Every effort has been made to trace copyright holders and obtain their
permission for the use of copyright material. The authors and publisher will
gladly receive information enabling them to rectify any error or omission in
subsequent editions. All facts are correct at time of going to press.

Published by Collins
An imprint of HarperCollins*Publishers* Ltd
1 London Bridge Street
London SE1 9GF

HarperCollins*Publishers*
Macken House, 39/40 Mayor Street Upper,
Dublin 1, D01 C9W8, Ireland

© HarperCollins*Publishers* Limited 2024

ISBN 9780008646462

First published 2024

10 9 8 7 6 5 4 3 2

British Library Cataloguing in Publication Data.

A CIP record of this book is available from the British Library.

Author: Sally White
Publisher: Sara Bennett
Editor: Shelley Teasdale
Cover Design: Sarah Duxbury and Kevin Robbins
Inside Concept Design: Sarah Duxbury and Paul Oates
Text Design and Layout: Jouve India Private Limited
Production: Bethany Brohm
Printed in Great Britain by Ashford Colour Press Ltd.

This book contains FSC™ certified paper and other controlled
sources to ensure responsible forest management.

For more information visit: www.harpercollins.co.uk/green